SIR GARY

SIR GARY
A Biography

TREVOR BAILEY

with a foreword by Richie Benaud

COLLINS
St James's Place, London
1976

William Collins Sons & Co Ltd
London · Glasgow · Sydney · Auckland
Toronto · Johannesburg

First published 1976
© Trevor Bailey 1976

ISBN 0 00 216764 6

Set in Monotype Baskerville
Made and Printed in Great Britain by
William Collins Sons & Co Ltd, Glasgow

To the late Sir Frank Worrell
who epitomised all that is best
in West Indian Cricket

Contents

Acknowledgments

I would like to thank my brother, Basil, for his care in checking the original copy and for unsplitting numerous infinitives, my daughter-in-law, Jackie, for her racing job on the typewriter, and Gary's numerous friends and relations who supplied me with the information without which the book could never have been written, and to Gary and Pru, for so patiently answering my many questions.

I am also grateful to Richie Benaud for providing the foreword. It is generally agreed that he was the most PR-conscious captain Australia has ever had. His post-match interviews for the press were brilliant, the only complaint I have encountered being from a journalist who felt that Richie also wanted to write his copy! I must also thank Jim Coldham for providing the index and discovering several inaccuracies, and David Frith for some helpful suggestions over photographs. Finally, I am indebted to Richard Cohen, who combined the jobs of editor and slave-driver most effectively, and whose enthusiasm for the project quelled some of my own doubts.

Illustration Credits

Foreword

by Richie Benaud

The trouble with writing a foreword about a great cricketer is that all his exploits are well-known; there is nothing new under the sun where someone like Sobers is concerned. Reading through the present book, I am delighted to see that Trevor has got him right – good things, demerit marks and all. It is a splendid chronicle of a man who is already a legend in the game. Yet I know Trevor Bailey will forgive me if I say that I detect a touch of irony in the fact that he is writing a book on Sir Garfield Sobers. Association of ideas is an interesting thing, and when I was asked to write this foreword my mind flashed immediately to Brisbane 1960, and then the association of ideas took it to Brisbane 1958.

The first was the occasion of Sobers scoring 132, a great innings in the famous 'Tied Test', made in fairly brisk time. The second was Trevor's 68 in seven hours two years earlier. Yet Australians in the Fifties know they would have had far more success against England had it not been for the author's wide defensive bat at the opposite end to a strong bowling attack. They know, too, that they would obviously have had more successes against the West Indies but for Sobers's presence. My own most vivid memory of Sobers is the first time he opened the batting for the West Indies in a Test Match, in the series against Australia in 1955. I was in that match, and had the pleasure of standing at gully throughout Gary's innings. It was particularly memorable because the West Indies were faced with a vast task – they were chasing an Australian total of 668. Their openers were Gary and J. K. Holt, a sleepy-eyed, cultured stroke-player who was a much better batsman than his figures in that series showed. When Gary was out, the first to go, caught at mid-wicket off Ian Johnson in the Australian captain's first over, he had scored 43 out of a total of 52. To watch that innings was a memorable experience – and for more than one reason.

When it began, late in the afternoon, Lindwall and Miller knew they could give everything, particularly as that delightful Barbados breeze was blowing across the ground, and so helping the bowlers. One over I lasted, then I said to Ian Johnson: 'Won't be a sec, Skip, just got to get something from the dressing rooms.' Now there have been all kinds of cartoons drawn depicting the value of the abdominal protector – ageing batsmen making funny remarks about 'Never needed to use one in my day', and so on. Humphrey Tilling once made the most amusing cricket speech I have heard on the same subject, so I make no excuse for having been cowardly enough to make the sojourn to the dressing room that day to slot in the well-known receptacle for cuff-links and press studs. Fielding as close in as I was, I had never before seen a ball consistently go so fast past me. I never saw it go so fast again; certainly that was the only time my courage needed the bolstering influence of protective equipment.

No, I will never forget that day; and obviously I will never forget the batsman, because of what he did from that day onward. Ironically he was twelfth man in the first Test in that series, a piece of selection which in itself was bewildering but which may have come about because of the injury to Jeff Stollmeyer just before the start of the game. Denis Atkinson was probably listed to be twelfth man, but instead he had to act as replacement captain and it was Sobers who had to carry the drinks.

All-rounders come in different styles, in different teams and in different eras. One of the most intriguing subjects for discussion in any cricketing circle is to name the greatest

all-rounder of the time, or indeed of all time. Trevor goes
for Gary. So do I, and I think only some biased octogenarian
would have another nomination. But I have always said,
and I say again, that Keith Miller was the greatest all-
rounder with whom I ever played. As a player, I only saw
Gary in that 1955 series in the West Indies, then in the 'Tied
Test' series in Australia. He was a great player, and he
continued his dynamic cricket in Australia when he came
to play Sheffield Shield cricket in the early Sixties. Miller
I played with in New South Wales from 1948 till 1956, and
in the Test side from 1951 to 1956, and he always seemed a
great cricketer and captain. I guess it is all a question of
being close to a cricketer. If someone asked me to name the
players who in the past quarter of a century have made
cricket worthwhile – worth watching and worth playing –
there are quite a few who would not get a guernsey. A very
short list of those who have done so would certainly include
both Sobers and Miller. I have always rated Miller this
highly. Perhaps I have some kind of psychological leaning to
the flamboyant, the unpredictable, the gambling aspect of
the game, even though the game is made up of administrators
and commentators as well as players, and they all have their
own patterns of play and behaviour. But Miller taught me
more about cricket than any other cricketer.

When in 1961 I began covering Test series for the media
I had the chance to watch Sobers from outside the fence.
He gave me more pleasure than any other man in the game,
and perhaps that is the measure of his standing – the ability
to give pleasure to all those watching, even those playing
against him. Yet even more important to me is the fact that
Gary wanted to give that pleasure. He is a born entertainer
as a cricketer, and if you tot up the pleasure millions of
cricket-watchers have derived from sitting at the ground,
watching on television, listening to the radio or reading
newspaper reports about him, then everyone owes him

something. He did more things well than other all-rounders. Some of us bowled well, batted reasonably, fielded well close to the wicket; others were outstanding batsmen, good bowlers, great outfielders. If we had to turn our hand to something strange, like bowling leg-breaks, off-breaks, cutters, swing with the new ball, open the innings, bat at seven, field at first slip, short leg, in the covers or on the boundary, something would be lacking. It hardly needs emphasising here that 'Sobey' could do it all.

Trevor explains all this in his book, but also makes the innuendo, which intrigues me, that there was a time when if Benaud bowled a googly then Sobers might not pick it. The same thing has been said about other great players over the years – Neil Harvey, for example, who had the reputation of not being able to pick the leg-spinner's googly. Like Sobers, he had no need to. When Gary says there were times when Subhash Gupte, the Indian leg-spinner, worried him, or that Benaud, the Australian leg-spinner, worried him, I treat it with the same quirk of the lips as when I hear that any particular bowler had the 'wood' on Bradman.

Sobers and Gupte met in India in the 1958/59 series on pitches which may well have assisted spin more than any other type of bowling. Sobers made 25, 142 not out, 4, 198 run out, 106 not out, 29, 9, and 44. Subhash dismissed him once. In the 'Tied Test' series he made 132, 14, 9, 0, 168, 1, 1, 20 run out, 64 and 21. I got him twice. I may have picked him up a couple of times in other matches over the years, but he didn't need to be able to pick top spinners or wrong 'uns. Most of the time he picked the ball off the pitch, and his defence was so sound and orthodox that there was never any daylight between bat and pad for the ball to squeeze through. Gary once said that he regarded his century in the 'Tied Test' as his best innings against Australia. I would agree with that. There is a film on show in Australia these days, a breakdown of shots he played in the Rest of the World XI match against Australia in Melbourne in 1972. The film is breathtaking, but I haven't the slightest doubt that if anyone cared to do a breakdown of that 'Tied Test' century the same magnificent strokes would be on show.

When he came in that day I was bowling from the Stanley Street end and I beat him with a top spinner. 'Beat him', that is, in the matter of whether or not he picked the delivery. The ball was pitched on a good length and it landed in a line drawn to middle and off stump. If it managed to evade his bat, I knew it was going to hit the off stump. Gary thought it was a leg-spinner, and he calmly was pushing it to mid-on, wide of my left hand, when it hit the pitch and hurried straight on. I was half-way through what was to pass for an exultant shout when the ball flashed past me to the boundary. It was a most unorthodox shot. He had flicked his wrist at the ball, simply changed the direction of the stroke but, incredibly, hadn't bothered to play it defensively. How he did it I will never know, nor will any of the players close to the wicket that day. They all rated it the shot of the innings and, in an innings of that kind, that is saying something.

One story I didn't know was where Trevor relates that the manager of the side in Sydney, the day I dismissed Gary in the state match before the Test, had said to him, 'Never mind, son, you will be able to pick him one of these days.' I think the manager that day is now the present Secretary of the Australian Cricket Board, Mr A. R. Barnes – and I will be having a word with him as soon as possible.

It reminds me of the day Bradman and Mailey were playing in a charity game at Blackheath, a town just outside Sydney in the Blue Mountains. At breakfast on the morning of the game Mailey picked up the paper and saw the headline right across the top of the page 'Mailey to defeat Bradman.' He got up from the table saying that he didn't

S.G.–B

feel hungry any more. 'I know exactly what is going to happen today once the little fellow reads this,' he was reported to have said. Bradman hit a very quick 100 in something like 39 minutes that day; and he reserved most of the punishment for Mailey.

In that 'Tied Test' Gary was bowling toward the end of the final day and, reading Trevor's research into his childhood and teenage years and what a good temperament he had even then, I can believe that those early days had a real influence on him keeping his head that day. Late in the afternoon, when Alan Davidson and I were in partnership, Sobers was bowling and bowling very well. He was in his medium pace role that afternoon, left-arm over the wicket and straight at middle stump, just short of driving length – with no singles during the over or at the end of the over to that tight-set field. He knew what he was trying to do, and it was his accuracy and good temperament that brought the frustration which in the end caused the first run out when Joe Solomon hit Davidson's stumps from mid-wicket. There was nothing wrong with Sobers's nerve that afternoon. He went around the wicket, then over again, and each time the sight-screens had to be moved, much to the vocal annoyance of the crowd behind the screen at the Stanley Street end. After three singles and three sight-screen shiftings, he changed his mind in mid-stride as the attendant was half-way through his next moving exercise, and the crowd really gave him the razz. 'Go on,' I said over the tumult, 'I bet you are not game to have it moved back again.' He just grinned. 'How much?' he said. I was the one who reneged. 'Forget it, they'll be over the fence,' I said hastily. As Trevor relates, Gary has always been one to take up a bet, even in later years!

When the West Indies came to Australia in 1960 we had been through two tours where, not to put too fine a point on it, the cricket had been slow. The previous tour by MCC had offered Brisbane crowds a few records they did not want, from Australian players as well as the touring side. Three of the days' play that summer in Brisbane are listed now as among the slowest in the history of the game. Brisbane cricket followers had a lot to make up. They have an affinity now for West Indian cricketers for, in 1960, they rejuvenated the game in that northern state. It was the freak result, of course, but in this sense it was secondary to the play which had been so refreshing that crowds have since flocked back to the game. So when Gary came back to Australia the following year he was given a great welcome. For that matter he has been given a great welcome everywhere he has gone; he is the real international cricketer, belonging to everyone.

In this period it was fascinating to take part in a match between New South Wales and South Australia and to watch two great left-hand all-rounders – Sobers and Alan Davidson – in action. Sobers made all the difference to South Australia, and he even managed to stand up to the gruelling amount of work handed out to him by skipper Les Favell. When he played his first season, South Australia just failed to win the Sheffield Shield, even though he scored a thousand runs for the summer and took fifty wickets. The following year, when he hit his six centuries, they made no mistake, and the Sheffield Shield came back to the state for the first time since 1953.

He and Davidson had some great battles, and it is interesting to reflect on their styles, as listed by Trevor in later pages. I played against Davidson as a fifteen-year-old schoolboy, when he was a left-arm, over-the-wrist spinner. The next year he also bowled left-arm orthodox spin! The following year he took the new ball for a Sydney first grade club, a year after that he was in the New South Wales Sheffield Shield team, and a year later in the Australian team which toured New Zealand. I doubt though that

Davidson would have been able to combine all those styles in one complete bowling pattern, as Sobers did. In fact, Davo's biggest problem was that from 1958 onward he had a captain who needed him to bowl fast from the start of play to the end of the day, in a period where Australia's pace bowling resources were at a low ebb. The great thing about watching Sobers and Davidson was the tremendous competitive aura – both great cricketers and never a moment when either would give in. I would mark down the cricketing battles between these two men as one of the everlasting memories in my cricket life.

I had finished my playing days when Gary became captain of the West Indies. I watched him lead them to a resounding victory in the Caribbean over Australia in 1965, then through England in 1966 and in Australia in 1968/69. To my mind, Trevor's assessment of him as a skipper is accurate, although I would add that I have always believed the loss of Frank Worrell had an effect on this aspect of Gary's career. Frank was one of the great men of the game, and it would have made a big difference in 1968/69 if Frank had been there as the 'father-figure' behind the scenes. Gary *did* become removed from the hard, grinding business of winning matches, and to everyone sitting by their radios a thousand miles away that is what the game is about. The reason he did this is exactly as Trevor describes. Although, if possible, Gary preferred to be on top, winning or losing is not, and never will be, the beginning or the end of the world for him.

A lot of people will tell you there are more important things in the world than cricket. Quite right. People, for example, are more important, the people taking part and those making themselves a part of it by off-the-field participation. I can understand Gary's annoyance and disappointment over the Rhodesian affair and its political overtones. If his political critics had done as much for people in their life as Sobers has done in his then we might all live in a better world. I hope now he has retired that he will continue to put effort into the game. He is too good a thinker on cricket and human relations to have his ability wasted in retirement. Perhaps he will turn to politics, perhaps, as mentioned, to representation as an ambassador, but I suspect secretly he would most like to be a top-class golfer. Perhaps as one of those cricketing 'bandits' Trevor mentions in Chapter 17, I might be able to get my foot on his money. Even on Trevor's, for that matter, if he has heeded the advice offered him by that canny, low-handicapper, Sir Leonard Hutton. But that is for the future. For the moment it is enough to salute the story of Sobers – great cricketer, great guy.

Author's Preface

A word about the form of the book. After writing of Gary's early years I abandoned a strictly chronological order, since neither his life nor his qualities as a cricketer can best be appreciated by that approach. I have, anyway, little regard for dates or statistics on their own: a century or a fine bowling performance means little and proves even less until set in its proper context.

I am also aware that I may be accused of having been too sympathetic to Gary, almost of hagiography. Yet I could not have presented his life in any other way. I have always admired him both as a cricketer and a person, and while writing this book my admiration for him increased. Yet I am confident I have not exaggerated. Should anyone feel my praise is mistaken I would suggest they ask anyone who knows Gary, or who has played cricket with him, what he is like. They will discover that Gary is that rarity – a man without malice or meanness.

Throughout his career Gary has had his name spelt with one 'r' and two. He would probably prefer the spelling 'Garry', but he is not seriously worried which form is used. I have therefore adopted the shorter version, in which I follow both the souvenir booklet produced for Gary's Benefit in the West Indies and that final arbiter of cricketing questions, *Wisden*.

Westcliff, January, 1976   TREVOR BAILEY

1

First Encounter

I was Gary Sobers's first Test victim. The moment came in the Fifth Test at Sabina Park, Jamaica, the concluding match of the highly controversial MCC tour to the West Indies in 1954. This game has always had a special significance for me not only because it contained my best-ever performance with the ball in international cricket but because, by winning, we squared the series, even though we had lost the first two Tests.

It was not an easy trip. Apart from the considerable ability of our opponents, politics and sport had become sadly entwined. England had wrested the Ashes from Australia the previous summer, so the series between England and the West Indies was looked upon by many as the unofficial world championship. This should merely have increased the cricketing interest, but as a number of the West Indian islands had just gained their independence the encounters took on a political and racial significance which our players had never had to face before.

With Brian Statham injured we decided to gamble on winning the toss, rely on two seam bowlers, Freddy Trueman and myself, and hope that our spin trio of Tony Lock, Jim Laker and Johnny Wardle would bowl the West Indies out in their second innings. When Sir Len Hutton called incorrectly and we went out to field with the pitch looking more grey than green in the brilliant sunlight, I thought a draw was about the best we could hope for. After all, in the previous Test the West Indies had scored 681 for 8 declared, and all the famous W's – Worrell, Weekes and Walcott –

had scored centuries. The one outcome none of us expected was that I would take 7 wickets for 34, that the West Indies would be back in the pavilion for 139, and that I would have the rare, possibly unique, experience of opening both England's bowling and batting on the same day in the Caribbean.

My partner was Len Hutton, and we were still together at close of play. On the following morning we survived a fusillade of bouncers from Frank King, at that time the Number One West Indian fast bowler. I ducked, dived and weaved, while Len smiled approvingly at me from the other end. Then, the shine having completely departed, Gary came on to bowl for the first time. In those days he was a very accurate left-arm orthodox slow bowler, with a high, classical delivery. He was not a big spinner of the ball, and on that perfect pitch even Alf Valentine, whose place he had taken, would have had difficulty in achieving any turn.

This was the first time I had played against Gary, and I was happy to see him come on as third change, because I have always preferred facing bowlers who aim to make the ball leave the bat. With the England total 43, Gary dropped one fractionally short outside my off stump. I could not resist the square cut, only to discover it was his arm-ball, with the result that I was too close and was snapped up behind the wicket. Bailey c. McWatt b. Sobers 24.

In England's first innings total of 414, which included a masterly double century by Len Hutton, Gary was not only very tidy, but captured four wickets. It was a most impressive performance, taking into account the plumb pitch, the small, fast outfield, his youth and his lack of experience. It confirms my view that had Gary possessed no batting potential he would still have developed into an orthodox left-arm spinner of international calibre. He had a smooth basic action, good control, a naturally deceptive flight and an equable approach to the job – all by the time he was seventeen. Knowing his dedication and determination to do well, I am sure he would have mastered all the variations of flight and increased his powers of spin, had these been his principal objectives. Of other left-arm slow bowlers only Derek Underwood, in an entirely different style, has impressed me as much at an early age.

Although Gary had batted at number 5 for Barbados and – remembering he was only 17 – had scored an impressive 40 against us, he was picked for the West Indies primarily as a slow bowler. All the same, I suspect that their selectors, with a draw sufficient to guarantee them the Rubber, were not averse to strengthening still further an exceptional batting line up with Gary at number 9. Gary's own reaction was mixed – on the one hand he was delighted, but, on the other, he was surprised to have achieved what was then his major ambition at such an early age. This was the only time in his career he was to gain his place in the West Indies side solely as a slow left-armer.

In this Test Gary was also to give a brief glimpse of his fine temperament and his potential with the bat. He came to the crease with the West Indian first innings in ruins, yet he still might have staged one of these special rescue acts for which he was to become so famous, had he not run out of partners and been left undefeated with 14. This tall, slim teenager had in fact looked far more comfortable than most of his seniors, and seemed quite unperturbed by the situation or occasion. As it was, neither the press in the West Indies nor in England picked up the significance of his début – it was lost in the general excitement of the match as a whole.

My next encounter with Gary was in 1957, in England, by which time his batting genius had been recognised, and he, Rohan Kanhai and Collie Smith were being spoken of as the natural successors to the three W's. By then his spin bowling was regarded as simply an additional bonus. A few years later he made the highest-ever Test score –

365 against Pakistan – and went on to become the most travelled, and most complete all-rounder the world has ever seen.

Besides developing into a magnificent batsman in all conditions and on all types of wicket, and being a useful slow left-armer, he added two more turns to his repertoire. He became a brilliant new ball pace bowler and a wrist-spinner of international calibre. There have been many great cricketers, but none has ever displayed such a vast range of talents before such a wide audience without ever losing his intense passion for the game.

For more than twenty years I bowled against the finest batsmen in the world and batted against the best bowlers, which has provided me with the ideal platform from which to judge their ability. I can also claim to have a special understanding and appreciation for my own kind, the all-rounders. Certainly nobody can hold Gary in higher regard as a cricketer. He has, quite simply, been the greatest of all time, the most complete all-rounder ever, with the figures to substantiate the claim.

He has not needed a big mouth, or a high-powered publicity campaign; the statistics alone are breath-taking. In Test matches he has scored 8,620 runs for an average of 58·63, taken 256 wickets at 33·01 apiece, and held 117 catches. In all first-class cricket his figures read: 28,315 runs, average 54.87, 143 wickets, average 27.74, and 407 catches.

Yet these figures, superb as they are, do less than justice to the finest cricketer I have ever played with or against. No all-rounder has ever approached them. For one thing they would have been even more remarkable had he been average-conscious, but Gary was quite rightly never interested in statistics for their own sake. His first concern has always been, both as player and as captain, for the game and not the individual.

Figures cannot convey the style and the elegance with

which the deeds were done, nor the presence of the man. He was not only a superb craftsman, but also a magnificent entertainer, who epitomised the best in cricket. His career is packed with outstanding performances in every facet of the game, and these were accomplished with a panache that makes them more memorable than most. He had that stature, or star quality, which typifies the great artist, be he sportsman, singer or actor. Whether he was batting, bowling or fielding he attracted followers with a magnetism which stemmed from the man himself as much as from his skill as a performer.

Gary was also a tremendous competitor who did much to destroy the myth that the West Indies are only good when on top. Backing up the ability and the natural laughter of the West Indians was a singleness of purpose which would not have been out of place in Yorkshire. Although he preferred to hit his way out of trouble with a cavalier counter-attack he was always prepared to graft his way to safety if the situation demanded it.

Having batted against Gary in all his three styles, having bowled against him many times and played with him and under his captaincy, having lost my wicket to him and returned the compliment, and having watched him so often from the commentary box, it was inevitable that I should have an immense regard for him as a cricketer. But that was not sufficient reason for writing this book. I would never have considered the task had I not liked and admired him as a man.

I know Gary, his wife and family and the West Indies rather better than most. I have been out to the Caribbean on seven occasions, have played with and against all their finest players since the war, and in 1964 even had the rare distinction of managing a West Indian team captained by Sir Frank Worrell on a short tour to England.

Gary was born with an inordinate amount of natural

ability, which, combined with his driving ambition to
succeed and an unruffled temperament – he was adult in
outlook even in his teens – guaranteed he would become one
of the game's immortals. He would have been outstanding
at almost any sport he chose to pursue. It is no surprise to
find that, in addition to cricket, he has represented Barbados
at soccer, basketball and golf, while table-tennis, tennis and
athletics came so easily to him that he could have excelled
at any of the three. He was athletically endowed, not merely
a brilliant ball player.

Fortunately for cricket Gary was born in Barbados, where
the game has an almost religious significance, and he
remained loyal to his first love. As he broke one record after
another with bat, ball and in the field, he was still able to
retain his natural charm and gaiety. This engaging trait plus
his innate sportsmanship and sense of fair play is why he is
universally held in such high esteem. In the cricket world,
which is often extremely bitchy, I have never come across
anybody who did not like him as a person and respect him
as a player. This applies just as much to his opponents,
perhaps more so, because some of his West Indian colleagues
became a little jealous of his success.

I have known Gary as a cricketer for over twenty years
and later, and even more rewarding, as a personal friend.
He is not, and makes no claim to be, a paragon of virtue,
which is as well because saints outside the Church are liable
to be boring. He has many human frailties. These include a
passion for gambling, a positive dislike of answering letters, a
certain unreliability, a firm belief that 'girls were made to
love and kiss' and, for a period, he had a tendency to drink
too heavily. However, these weaknesses fade into insigni-
ficance when considered against his extraordinary zest for
living, his infectious laugh, the complete absence of side – so
that he is at home in any company – and his absolute
honesty in everything he says or does.

2
Childhood in Barbados

Barbados is unlike most of the islands in the Caribbean. Until its independence was granted in 1966 it remained a British possession. The majority of its neighbours changed hands several times. In Jamaica traces of Spanish culture exist, while there is a very marked French influence in St Lucia. Barbados, however, stayed especially close to the Mother Country and became known as 'Little England'.

Before the Second World War, Barbados might best have been described as a 'benevolent plantocracy' with colonial undertones, or perhaps as a 'benign oligarchy', democratic in design rather than degree. The population could be easily divided into a number of ethnic and social sections. The white colonial administrators, headed by the Governor General, were English, and in the main both honest and fair. Most came to love the island, but their home was always England, and their outlook was basically conservative. Not without cause, they viewed every change with suspicion. They were in the main transient, but there was also a small, élite group of white Barbadians, many of whom were descendants of the original plantation owners and overseers. This point was driven home to me when, having lunch with Captain Wilf Farmer, the policeman who was to play such an important part in Gary's early career, I asked him how long he had lived in Barbados. I should have known better; nobody who has not been there for a very long time can acquire that distinctive accent, but I was surprised to learn that his ancestors had settled there some three hundred years before.

Because of the smallness of Barbados this powerful white minority had sensibly diversified their interests from the sugar cane industry, which was their main source of revenue, to property, trade and business on the island. In this period tourism, now the major industry, was in its infancy.

A certain number of white newcomers, providing they had enough money and were socially acceptable, were regularly taken into what was really a tightly-knit aristocracy based on colour, wealth and background. There was also a middle-class white element, never quite able to bridge the gap, or be accepted for the Yacht Club. That left the poor whites, unwanted and despised by everyone, and the 'Red Legs', direct descendants of prisoners sent out during the Cromwellian Wars. The latter, a dying species, had gone native over the years and lived largely by fishing.

The black population had also established its own élite society, which in many respects was more difficult to enter than that of the whites. It contained the most successful doctors, lawyers, politicians – providing they were not radical – and businessmen. They had wealth and brains, and their children were well educated. Their cricket club was called 'the Spartans'. It was so exclusive that a black man without the correct connections and background had little chance of being accepted as a member. The Empire Club was a direct result of the exclusiveness of the predominately light-skinned Spartans. Beneath this top echelon was a large, respectable and law-abiding middle- and lower-middle class. It contained minor government officials, store keepers, schoolmasters, police and bank clerks; those who had moved ahead – or at least felt they had – of the plantation and domestic workers, who made up the bulk of the coloured population.

Nobody could claim that it was a perfect society. There were many inequalities, but the interesting fact is that the people as a whole were far happier than in many lands

1 The young Test cricketer—Gary Sobers in 1955.

2 Domino-playing in the West Indies — one of Gary's first 'sporting' successes.

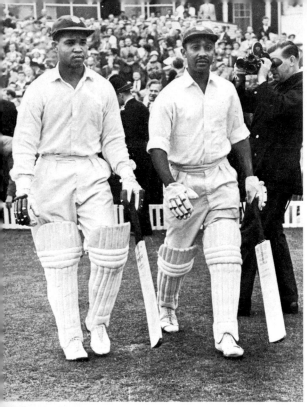

3 Gary walks out with Frank Worrell – a major influence in his life – to open the West Indies innings in the fourth Test at Leeds in 1957.

4 Gary with his closest friend, O.G. Smith, in May 1957.

where the inequalities are less. Although exploitation of the semi-illiterate dark man by both the white and those of his own colour was once blatant in Barbados, it was not as bad as in other parts of the world. Indeed, at the time there were few who saw it as exploitation.

I was talking to a leading Barbadian politician about the happiness that clearly existed in his island despite conditions and situations which today would be considered in the favourite words of every trade union official as 'totally unacceptable'. He put forward the idea that a man with cancer can be content, providing he is unaware of the cause. It is easy to understand his argument; but the coloured worker was neither dying, nor in pain. The overwhelming impression gained from interviews with Gary, his brothers and his friends was that, although they would have been considered underprivileged by today's standards, their childhood was exceptionally happy. Contentment stems from a state of mind rather than from money or material possessions.

Gary was born on 28 July 1936, at 3.30 a.m., in a small wooden house in Walcott's Avenue, Bay Land, St Michael, Barbados, where Mrs Thelma Sobers lived with her husband and four other young children. It was and still is an un-exceptional road in an unpretentious area; clean, but certainly not prosperous. Gary became the fifth child in a typically large West Indian family. The only unusual feature was that his parents should have christened him Garfield St Aubrun – which, following George, Greta, Elise and Gerry, does appear an exotic choice.

His father was a handsome merchant seaman with a reputation for smart dressing and a love of life. Although his wages were small they were higher than those of the average plantation worker. There was no money for luxuries, but his family were happy, well fed and adequately clothed. They were liked and respected in the neighbourhood and his home was perpetually full of laughter, noise and children.

Like the majority of West Indians, particularly 'Bajans', as Barbadians are known, his three sons quickly developed a love of cricket and, though no great performer himself, he was only too pleased to encourage them, and when home on leave he would spend hours playing with them. In the early days most of the cricket took place at the side of the house, in the field at the back – no longer there – and in the streets, which carried little traffic apart from bikes. As if this was not enough, the boys brought the game into the little house – a venue which did not have the complete approval of Mrs Sobers.

Gary was weaned on a diet of cricket from the age of three. There were always two brothers on hand to play with, while sometimes his two sisters were drafted in, if only to provide additional fielders. That the bats were crude affairs and the balls often a compound of tar and rags in no way detracted from the fun. Gary himself recalls those far off days with obvious affection and not a little nostalgia.

Mrs Sobers was to have another son, Cecil. A seventh child died shortly after birth. Then, suddenly and dramatically, this boisterous, contented family were confronted by a major tragedy. On 11 January 1942 the *Lady Drake*, in which Gary's father was serving, was torpedoed as it was bringing supplies to Barbados. It went down with all hands. Mrs Sobers found herself faced with the considerable task of bringing up six young children on her own. She accepted the challenge with courage and fortitude, and proceeded to devote the rest of her life to being both father and mother to them.

This remarkable woman succeeded magnificently. She spared herself nothing in seeing they not only had a real home but were raised in a practical, Christian fashion. They were taught to be honest, truthful and generous, and to have respect for herself and others. She had always been a regular church-goer, and she undoubtedly drew comfort and strength from her faith. In the early days her children would accompany her to church, immaculately turned out, as they always are throughout the West Indies – I have never come across cleaner, better- or more gaily-dressed youngsters than in the Caribbean on Sundays. Mrs Sobers still sits in the same pew, but, as her family grew up and became more independent, their own attendances decreased.

There are numerous problems for even the most determined of women in rearing such a large family on a small widow's pension, but they were to some extent lessened because she lived in Barbados. First, nobody on the island should starve, as there is an abundance of fruit, plenty of fish and no real shortage of basic foods. Second, a minimum of clothing is required in that permanently pleasant climate. Third, in the Forties at any rate, there was a genuine community spirit. This is always preferable to any government welfare scheme, because it is based on compassion, affection and real interest in the recipients, who do not regard it as a right. Thus although her neighbours did not have all that number of worldly possessions they were only too willing to try to help the young widow. They were poor, but there was no poverty. There is a world of difference between the two.

Children are extremely resilient in the face of death, and with their mother hiding her emotions within herself, there was little change in the Sobers's household once the initial shock had passed. The young are too busy and too involved in their own lives to mourn for long. Their adventures at school, the games they played, their friends and the fun continued, while their mother was always available as provider and comforter. She encouraged her sons' passion for cricket, for it kept them happy and out of mischief, even if the occasional window was broken. What never occurred to her as she watched them bat and bowl from early morning until dusk was that Gary was taking his first hesitant steps toward stardom.

Mrs Sobers was a good and careful housekeeper, indeed she could not afford to be anything else. Her aim was to make sure that her family had sufficient wholesome food, which they did. Each morning started with the preparation of six substantial breakfasts. She would then make sure these were eaten and that the children left both clean and on time for school, where they usually had a snack lunch. In the evening she would cook a meal, in which one of the main ingredients was normally rice to go with the fish, chicken or meat. Rice has become a staple diet in the West Indies and it remains a great favourite with Gary, who still has it on every possible occasion.

In between getting twenty-one meals each day she kept her small, single-storey house spotless, tried to do the same but with considerably less success for her offspring, made some of their clothes, never stopped mending them, shopped with care, and occasionally allowed herself the luxury of sitting down for five minutes. After the death of her husband she 'never looked at another man' (her children's comment), and literally lived for her children.

What was Gary like as a child? His mother says that, apart from his obsession with all sports, he was very normal, though old for his years. He seldom caused her any worry; neither did the rest of her brood, a tribute to her qualities as a mother. He always preferred games to work, though he had a natural head for figures. Once he was involved in a game of cricket he became oblivious to everything else. She tried to discourage his left-handedness, but fortunately failed. He possessed unlimited energy and, despite looking frail in his early youth, was always very fit.

Today Gary's mother is a slight, grey-haired lady with a ready smile. Like most Bajans, she talks so quickly and chuckles so frequently that it is difficult for a foreigner to understand all she says. She is never happier than with her children and grandchildren and still lives in the house where she raised them all. It has been modernised, enlarged and is now made of stone. It contains a priceless collection of Gary's cricket trophies and, as might be expected, is spotless.

When I was in Barbados gathering material on Gary's life, I called to see her with Gary and later went back with Gary's wife, Pru. This visit had to be done with considerable secrecy and without Gary's knowledge. ITV had asked me to do some research for their programme, 'This is Your Life', in which they intended to feature Gary. It was vital for his mother to come to England. Pru was worried that she might not be willing to make the journey, because she had never been out of Barbados in her life, and had never flown. Although Gary had often asked her to come to stay with him in England, she had always declined. Fortunately she agreed to our request – Pru is very persuasive – and she also managed to keep quiet about the whole project. This cannot have been easy for a normally chatty individual who was about to embark on what was a real adventure into the unknown. One wrong word and the whole story would have spread through that little island with the speed of a bush-fire. A remarkable woman.

3

The Young Cricketer

Gary's early interest in cricket was keen but the equipment was primitive. His bat was normally a wooden paling, the ball a crude affair, often made from tar and rags. But there was never any shortage of players; most West Indians, irrespective of age, are only too happy to take part. Pick-up games occurred in the street, on the beach, or indeed in any open space.

As Gary and his brothers grew older they were introduced to other forms of the game which they also found much to their taste – because these were sometimes organised, which increased the competitiveness. Two favourites were 'Little', or 'Small Ball' cricket, and 'Soft Ball', or 'Hopping Ball' cricket. In the former the batsman knelt on one knee and used a Lilliputian bat, while the size of the stumps and pitch was greatly reduced. The ball was usually of rubber or had a tar centre, and all the bowling was underarm. Little Cricket was very popular then in school breaks, and there were even organised leagues. With his ability to break the ball sharply, quick reactions and wonderful eye Gary soon established himself as one of the star performers. One of Gary's school friends, Armiston Brown, still recalls with awe the prodigious amount of spin that Gary was able to impart.

However, it was 'Soft Ball' cricket which was to have a considerable effect on Gary's subsequent career. This is basically normal cricket played with a tennis ball. In a pick-up game, as distinct from an organised match, there are liable to be a vast number of fieldsmen, which means the duration of each innings is inclined to be brief. With its high bounce a tennis ball is apt to be hit in the air, and there can well be twenty or thirty pairs of hands eagerly awaiting the catch.

This point soon registered in the cricket brain of the young Sobers, who, when batting, was confronted by the additional problem of being very small for his age. He realised that to stay at the wicket he had to learn to hit the rising ball along the ground with a straight bat, while in any cross-bat stroke it clearly paid to roll the wrists. These two fundamentals in the art of batsmanship were acquired by Gary at a very early age.

Another practical advantage of this kind of cricket for small boys is that there is no danger of being hurt. This means that they can learn the value of moving into line without any physical fear. The youngster who is unlucky enough to be reared on bad pitches against a hard ball is understandably apprehensive. He may be told the importance of getting behind each delivery, but should one rise and hit him the chances are that he will take to the habit of retreating toward the square leg umpire.

Soft Ball cricket leagues still flourish in Barbados and encourage a flow of young batsmen who instinctively move into line and are able to 'hit de ball on de rise', but still keep it along the ground. Gary is convinced that one of the reasons for his success as a batsman is the initial grounding he received batting against a tennis ball.

When Gary joined his brother, Gerry, at the Bay Street Primary School (now a ministerial building) he was lucky to encounter Everton Barrow as sports master. Everton was a good cricketer himself. He played for the Empire Club, was young and enthusiastic, and soon realised the potential of the two Sobers brothers, to whom he gave a great deal of encouragement.

Owing to the lightness of their skin, the elongation of their
eyes and their slight build, the pair became known as the
'Chinese brothers'. They were soon to make a big impact in
local schools cricket. 'Watch out, mun, or de two Chinee
boys will do you' was the oft-repeated warning of their
opponents.

Gerry became captain of the school cricket team. He was
also the principal batsman and wicketkeeper, while the
diminutive Gary bowled the other sides out. The Sobers
brothers were so much better than other boys of their age
that they proceeded to dominate primary school cricket with
their exploits. Understandably, they were regarded with
some awe by their contemporaries, and the fact that on
each hand Gary had the beginnings of an extra finger – he
was to have them removed later – added to the mysticism.
Twelve-fingered spinners are not common!

While at school and then after he left, at the age of thirteen,
Gary spent much time at the furniture-making workshop of
Lionel Daniel, a near-neighbour. Lionel enjoyed cricket
and also played football with his two brothers for Notre
Dame, one of the leading teams in Barbados. Gary was later
to join the same club, and, though he was a natural outside-
left, he gained his place as a goalkeeper. That he was capped
for Barbados in this position is hardly surprising, when one
thinks of his agility, catching and quick reactions as a
fielder.

Although Lionel did teach Gary the rudiments of carpentry
and often provided him with pocket-money, the big attraction of Lionel's establishment for Gary was that it happened
to overlook the Wanderers' cricket ground. When the boys
who congregated there tired of assisting in the little factory,
they were sent out to play cricket amongst themselves. The
Wanderers was an all-white club and a member of the
Barbados Cricket Association, which was, and still is,
responsible for all senior cricket on the island.

Their coloured groundsman, Briggs Grandison, loved the game and also played for the local Bay Land Cricket Club in the Barbados League. It did not take Briggs long to recognise the natural talent of the slim kid with the graceful bowling action, who was also so much better than anyone else when batting against a soft ball. In those days there was never a shortage of net bowlers. Any spectator was only too willing to oblige. Once Dennis Atkinson, a member of the Wanderers Club (and later to captain both Barbados and the West Indies), asked Briggs to get the little left-armer who was watching to come and bowl at him. Briggs approached Gary, who was rather scared at the request, but the boy's fears were quickly dispelled by the following words: 'Don't you worry, boy. Bowl at his left pad and I'll be fielding at mid off.' It is difficult to think of a more sensible piece of advice to give a nervous boy-bowler.

This was the start of many rewarding hours Gary spent bowling in the nets at club members. Atkinson remembers putting a shilling on each stump as an incentive to the bowlers to try to get him out and also to make himself concentrate to the maximum. Gary also told me it was Dennis who gave him his first proper bat. Within a few years Atkinson and Gary were to be playing together for the West Indies . . .

A good bowler must have an abundance of natural ability, but he will never master his craft unless he is prepared to work at it. This especially applies to a spinner. Without the hours he spent toiling away on good wickets against keen batsmen in the nets at the Wanderers it is unlikely Gary would have been chosen for Barbados at sixteen.

The day was now fast approaching for Gary to move from schoolboy and Soft Ball cricket into the adult game, and appropriately enough he started in the Barbados Cricket League, which was founded in 1937 by the late Mitchie

Hewitt and which has played an enormous part in the development of the game in Barbados.

From the League have come players like Everton Weekes, Seymour Nurse, Charlie Griffith, Keith Boyce and Gary himself, but what has in the long run been far more important is the immense amount of enjoyment it has provided for thousands of Barbadians, who, without the League, would never have known the joy and excitement of competitive cricket.

To appreciate what the League has done since its inception and the part played by cricket in the sociological development of Barbados, it is necessary to have an understanding of what life was like on this little island when it was part of a still-powerful Empire. It was very different from today. Gary's career and the position he now occupies in the world could never have occurred then. Had he been born in the early twenties, he would have become a great player, assuming he was given the opportunity, but he could never have reached his present status in both world and Barbadian society.

In the late Thirties and early Forties black and white met as equals on the cricket field. The game cut through the social barriers, even though a white captain was considered indispensible in first-class matches. Until the formation of the Barbados Cricket League a poor coloured boy, unless he went to a High School, had little chance of taking part in competitive cricket when he grew up. The League provided the opportunity for anybody with ability and also gave enormous pleasure to the many who simply wanted to take part in regular, organised games. These League matches were keenly fought, something to look forward to during the week and to talk about throughout the next. The grounds were usually small and bumpy, while the pitch was on a plateau, to prevent it sinking when watered and rolled. I was fascinated by one where the run-up for the bowler at one end was so steep that the non-striker needed to be informed by his colleague when the bowler was starting his run!

The obvious League Club for Gary to join was the one led by Briggs Grandison, but it was felt that Gary was too small and might be hurt. It was also argued that he had plenty of time before joining a senior team, and that to include him meant somebody would have had to stand down.

His breakthrough into men's cricket occurred, in fact, by chance. The Bay Land team, under Briggs Grandison, was due to meet Kent, a country district side, in a friendly on a Sunday. Briggs found himself short of two players on the morning of the match, and decided to take along Gary and another youngster to make up the numbers.

Kent at that time was captained by Garnett Ashby, a builder and friend of Briggs who had already seen Gary performing at Soft Ball cricket. He was keen to show the team from the city that country cricket was strong, but the most significant feature of this meeting was that Garfield Sobers, a kid in short pants, was making his début in an adult match.

Gary was brought on as first change, and within a couple of overs two Kent batsmen were back in the pavilion. Skipper Garnett decided, quite logically, that this called for that violent counter-attack which has always been such a feature of West Indian cricket. He decided to go after the youngster in an effort to destroy both his length and his confidence. The intention was admirable, and, although the outcome was far from what he had intended, it filled him with both pain and pleasure. Twenty-five years later he can still recall the match with perfect clarity:

'I gave him de charge, mun. Twice it go over de boundary, but de third time it was not quite dare. Gary held it back a little, and I was out.'

Garnett was convinced that the boy was something

special, ripe for men's cricket, but, even more important, he decided to do something about it personally. He had seen other promising youngsters lose interest through lack of opportunity, and he was determined that this would not happen to Gary. As Garnett put it: 'The candle was there, all I needed to do was to strike the match.'

Garnett's first step was to ask whether Gary would like to play regularly for Kent in the country districts section of the Barbadian League, and the cricket-mad boy naturally jumped at the chance. The next step was more difficult. Garnett had to persuade Mrs Sobers to give her permission. The Kent ground was situated in the delightfully named 'Penny Hole', and, though this was only some twelve miles from Gary's home, it was in those days both remote and inaccessible. Public transport was infrequent; in any case there was no money over in the Sobers family for bus fares. Even if Gary was able to reach the ground by bus – and in his first match he was put on it at 5 a.m., and then told to get off at the woods by Penny Hole, where Garnett was waiting – there was no way he could get back home the same night. Mrs Sobers was a tolerant mother, but she did not intend to have her son wandering around the island in the dark. However, Garnett was nothing if not persuasive. Nobody could possibly doubt his sincerity or his enthusiasm. He quietened the mother's fears by telling her that he intended to take Gary into his home and that he would be personally responsible for her son's welfare. The outcome was she lost Gary at weekends to Garnett, who gained another son for his already large family.

The final requirement was for Garnett to register his young protégé with the Barbados Cricket League. The founder, driving force and Secretary of the organisation, Mitchie Hewitt, was typically quick and helpful. Speed has never been the outstanding characteristic of the Caribbeans, but in less than a week Garnett had recognised genius, gained a mother's confidence, adopted a weekend son, registered him with the League and acquired a cricketer who was to play a considerable part in the success of Kent for the next year and a half.

Although it was not really remarkable that such a shrewd judge and cricket enthusiast as Garnett should immediately recognise genius, it was remarkable that Gary should have been born with so much natural talent. He did not come from a family with a great sporting tradition, and his father certainly had no pretensions of being a cricketer. However, his mother says that Gary's grandfather had been very keen on the game before he emigrated to America.

In their youth all four Sobers brothers were competent and enthusiastic players. George, who became the bread-winner at an early age and went to sea, never had the opportunity to realise his potential. Gerry, who at school was an outstanding batsman and a useful wicketkeeper, had the misfortune to come on the adult scene when Barbados was abounding with talented cricketers. He might otherwise have represented the Island, and did in fact have several seasons of League cricket in England without ever measuring up to his early promise. Cecil, the youngest, probably suffered from being brought up under the considerable shadow of Gary himself.

4

Breakthrough

Gary joined Kent as a slow left-arm bowler with admirable
control of line and length and a temperament to match.
These virtues were more than sufficient to guarantee success
at this level of cricket. The wickets were always liable to
be untrustworthy, giving a bowler some help, while the
boundaries were short, which meant that it was not vital
to be a big spinner. Indeed, it could on occasions be something of a handicap.

Two of his early performances against Sussex, then rated
among the stronger sides in the Country League, demonstrate
his effectiveness as an accurate left-armer – 6 for 20 out of an
opposition total of 52, and 8 for 17 out of a total of 39.
However, even more remarkable than his record was his
obvious maturity. He was barely thirteen and had never
played in competitive adult cricket before, but knew immediately where to bowl, how to bowl, and what field he
required.

Garnett, a keen and thoughtful captain, was fascinated
by the precocious cricket brain of his young protégé. The
outcome was that from the third game onward he allowed
Gary to set his own field, because the boy's judgment was
invariably good.

Lucky skipper, but also lucky Gary to find a captain who
was immediately prepared to allow him to use his own
initiative, but still there to guide and advise from time to
time. For instance, on a pitch which was receptive to spin,
which resulted in Gary beating the bat too much, Garnett
would suggest that he pushed the ball through a shade

quicker. But in the main he simply gave Gary his head and plenty of encouragement. He was delighted to see Gary go from success to success, and with rare foresight was convinced that he was helping to bring on somebody who one day would be the talk, not only of his little Country League, but of the whole cricket world.

For nearly two seasons, under Garnett, Gary was to create havoc and break records in this minor cricket. Initially he was used purely as a bowler. As his captain recalls, he did not want to bat and would even hide in the long grass to make sure that he would not be called upon to go to the crease. He was still so diminutive, the men so big, the ball so hard and the pitches so unpredictable that he was understandably apprehensive. This ended when one day Kent found themselves in serious trouble against local rivals. It was then that Garnett displayed a true captain's instinct and timing.

He knew Gary had the ability to make runs because he had seen him dominate schoolboy cricket; so with 38 needed and all the recognised batsmen out, he turned to the boy and said. 'Take my bat' – a much-cherished 'Don Bradman' bat – 'and don't you come back, mun, until we won.' The response was typical Sobers, a breathtaking six over the keeper, to be followed by a flurry of strokes. Victory came quickly, and without the need for any assistance from the other end.

From that moment Gary became an all-rounder for Kent, and showed it by deeds with both the bat and the ball. No longer was he fearful of batting – rather, he could not reach the middle quickly enough. He had tasted runs in adult cricket, and wanted more. At the end of the season he was chosen to take part in a representative match between the Country and the City Leagues. In this game he was to bowl his brother, Gerry, out for nought – there is no room for sentiment in cricket – and the time was fast approaching for him to move on into senior cricket. He had, however, to find a club. Once again fate smiled and another captain was on hand to guide his cricket destiny.

One Friday afternoon during the local season of 1952 Wilfred Farmer, later to be Commissioner of Police for Barbados, but then a Police Superintendent, happened to be walking round the Wanderers' ground where Gary was batting in a soft ball game. Wilfred was also captain of the police cricket team, a fine player in his own right who had scored a double century for the Island against Jamaica and might well have developed into an outstanding fast bowler had he not damaged his back. With his knowledge and love for the sport he could not fail to be impressed by the sight of the boy Garfield in full flow. He was captivated, and in an article on Gary in 1973 wrote:

'Talent such as that displayed by the young Sobers is so immediately impressive, so blatantly obvious to the eye of anyone with the merest grain of cricketing knowledge, that its early revelation to a wondering world was inevitable.

'The ability consistently to drive a tennis ball sizzling along the turf, to cut with absolute precision, and to execute a series of sophisticated, if traditional, shots marks a lad with the stamp of genius for all to see, and it becomes only a question of how soon.'

The captain of the Police XI was so fascinated by what he had been watching that he asked a local cricket follower for the name of the slim lad with the graceful style. He was told that the boy was the terror of the soft ball games.

Also present on that fateful Friday was Dennis Atkinson, who played for Barbados. He not only confirmed the boy's prowess with a soft ball, but told Wilfred, against whom he played regularly in club cricket, that the lad was also a left-arm spinner of enormous promise, who had often bowled against him in the nets.

5 Gary's first Test — and his first Test victim. Trevor Bailey, caught by the wicketkeeper, Clifford McWatt, for 24. The date was April Fool's Day, 1954.

6 The compliment almost returned. I just fail to run Gary out at Trent Bridge in 1957.

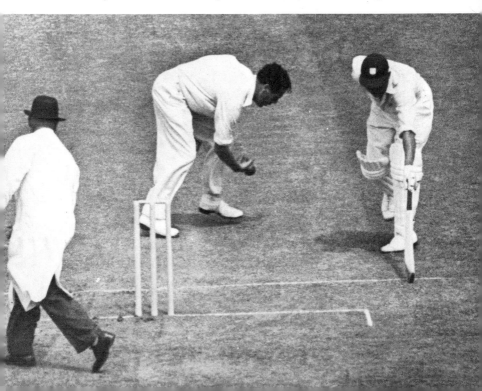

7 International recognition; Gary acknowledges the jubilation of the crowd as he reaches 300 during his record-breaking 365 not out against Pakistan in 1958.

8 In full cry: a drive-cum-slash off the front foot. The mature Sobers during the England v Rest of the World series of June 1970. Few batsmen have ever played this shot so well off pace bowling.

Wilfred Farmer instinctively knew, like Garnett Ashby before him, that he had been privileged to see a great player in embryo and that he must do something about it. The talent was there, but how could it be introduced to senior club cricket? He asked Tom Sealey, a local follower of cricket and a fan of Gary's, to bring the youngster over for a chat. His own words about this first meeting are especially interesting, because Wilfred was a white Bajan, whose ancestors had come to the Island some three hundred years before. He had been brought up there and must have seen thousands of promising coloured kids. He was also a trained, level-headed policeman, with a realistic, practical outlook.

'It was then,' he says, 'that it became even more obvious that here was a boy of promise. He was shy, yes, but there was none of the usual shrinking, simpering, tongue-tied reticence about him. He answered questions and volunteered information frankly and firmly. He bore himself manfully – not by any means mannishly – and met your eyes squarely and directly with no trace of suspicion or defiance.'

Wilfred was hooked. He promptly made a decision which was to have a considerable effect on Gary's career. Not only was this out of character; in the circumstances at the time it was remarkable. He asked the boy if he would like to join the police band and train to become a musician. Gary was neither very interested in nor talented at music. The real attraction was that the appointment made Gary eligible to play for the Police XI, who were members of the Barbados Cricket Association who chose the representative sides.

The following Monday, thanks to Wilfred's influence, Gary was enrolled in the police as a trainee. This provided him with a little pocket-money, but, what was far more important both to him and the sport, it enabled him to take part in a better class of cricket with much improved facilities and practice arrangements. If he could make the grade at that level he would automatically be seen by the Barbados selectors.

In an early game for the Police XI against Empire C.C. an incident occurred which, because of Gary's small size (he was then about 5 ft 4 ins) many in the Bay Land area had always feared might happen. He was facing a former West Indian fast bowler, Foffie Williams, and struck him for an effortless boundary. The reply was the usual bouncer. Gary attempted to hook, but the ball was a shade too quick and struck him in the face. This stopped him from practising the trumpet, which many of the more musically-minded considered a distinct advantage, but it had no adverse effect on his cricket, and he was able to take his place in the side on the following Saturday.

Wilfred Farmer's belief that Gary would quickly make his mark in senior club cricket was soon justified. From the outset Gary was always making valuable contributions with either the bat or the ball, generally both. Although he did not remain long with the band, he continued to play for the police because he had joined a youth club which was run by them. His first century was appropriately enough against the Wanderers, a very powerful side. His 113 not out was scored when all seemed lost, an innings which not only demonstrated his technique, but also his character.

In 1952 Gary was sixteen and already recognised as among the best all-rounders in the Island. Against the Lodege School XI, which played in the Barbados Cricket Association, he hit a hundred and captured nine wickets for 69 in their two innings. Feats like this brought him to the notice of the Barbados selectors. And by this time, too, he had grown to six foot. This late sprouting did not, as is often the case, spoil his flighting of the ball, or lead to any deterioration in his bowling skill. It was also a great asset to his batting. Despite his age he was summoned to trials with the Island team and chosen as twelfth man against the Indian touring side.

Again fate was at hand. On the morning of the match the West Indian selectors insisted on fast bowler Frank King being rested in order to keep him fresh for the next Test. As a result Gary was thrust into the Barbados XI – still at the age of sixteen. Typically, he seized the opportunity and returned the following figures: 22–5–50–4 and 67–35–92–3. Taking into account that this bowling was against international opposition on a wicket rightly considered among the best batting pitches in the world, and that it was by a boy making his début in first-class cricket, one can appreciate what a truly remarkable performance this was. Vijay Hazare, captain of India, where they appreciate spinners more than most, predicted that the youngster would become 'a great cricketer'. Gary had not only proved he possessed exceptional ability, he had displayed that essential ingredient for success at the top – the temperament for the big occasion.

The following season Gary was firmly established in the Barbados XI as their slow left-arm bowler and as a useful, hard-hitting, middle-order bat. With the three W's and a number of other fine run-getters in the team his opportunities at the crease were understandably limited, and it is not all that surprising that he was first capped for the West Indies as a spinner. It was not until the following year, when the Australians were making their first-ever tour of the Caribbean, that it finally dawned on everybody that Gary was much more than just an outstanding prospect.

I asked Clyde Walcott when he first realised Gary was something special. He immediately chose the Australian Test Match at Bridgetown in 1955. Although he knew Gary to be a good bowler, like most great batsmen he tended to regard all but the finest with something approaching condescension. The West Indies at that time were having difficulty

in finding an effective opening pair to face the pace of
Ray Lindwall and Keith Miller. The job was given to Gary,
who had been batting at No. 6 for both Barbados and the
National XI. He did not make a vast score, but his vicious
assault on the new ball in the hands of two great bowlers
was among the most spectacular ever seen. He included six
boundaries in his first 25 runs. Keith, one of the sufferers,
had this to say about the incident: 'In 1955 we simply
accepted Sobers as a left-arm orthodox spinner who was an
understudy to the great Alf Valentine. He didn't show us
anything out of the ordinary that would indicate what
brilliance was yet to come . . . Until Sobers was sent in to
open the West Indies innings. There, for an hour, cricket
hell broke loose. This little-known Sobers kept hammering
fours at Ray and myself until we were punch-drunk. That
one innings set Sobers alight as a batting wizard.'

In that Test series Gary showed that he was now an
international all-rounder, finishing second in the bowling
averages and having a batting average of 38. In the next
two decades he was to break record after record and to
bring a new dimension to the game.

5
Father-figures

One intriguing aspect of Gary's life has been the way he regularly acquired, both as a child and as a young man, a whole series of father-figures. Each took on their 'father role' instinctively, almost as if it were ordained. What was the special appeal Gary possessed? And why were so many men prepared to devote so much time to helping and guiding him?

There were obvious attractions in the early days. It is not easy to resist the charm of a graceful little boy with laughing eyes and an inborn talent for sport. That charm has never left Gary, and is as natural as his cricket ability. In addition, he was always old for his years and has consequently enjoyed, and been completely at home in, the company of older people. He was interested and keen to hear what they had to say. Devoid of malice, ambitious and talented, he represented as man and boy the type of son many a father would like to have.

The first and in many respects the most important of these mentors was Gordon Cumberbatch, who lived almost next door to where Gary was brought up and had been a close friend of his father. As a child Gary called him 'Dada', and indeed he still does. It was a close-knit community and naturally Dada tried to assist a large and fatherless family. The special relationship and deep affection which he felt for Gary manifested themselves in many ways. He became a father, a friend, an adviser and a confidant. His house became Gary's second home. He played cricket in the street with him, spent time on him, guided him along the

right lines and gave him love. Gary has never forgotten the
debt he owes Dada for what he did in those formative years.

It was Dada who taught Gary how to play dominoes.
In England this is a quiet, peaceful game, very popular in
some of the older pubs; in the West Indies it is a far more
boisterous affair, nearly always between two pairs, and
played with much noise and gusto. Its nearest English
equivalent would be darts. It is almost a national sport –
beloved in particular by taxi-drivers. Go to any taxi rank
and the chances are you will hear a lively game in progress.
There is always money at stake, and so for all the laughter
the game is taken seriously. Dada was an expert, famed for
his skill in Bridgetown. He did not suffer, indeed could not
afford, bad partners.

One day he was playing a friendly game at home with
George, Gary's eldest brother, who made so many errors
Dada was provoked into saying: 'I'll never play with you
again.' The fact that Gordon's wife was on the winning side
may have had something to do with his irritation. Nine-
year-old Gary was looking on. Immediately brother George
had been dismissed he opened his big brown eyes and asked
'Will you teach me dominoes, Dada?' Chances of refusing
that plea were nil.

The outcome of this successful request came as something
of a surprise to Dada, for Gary took to the game with all the
relish of a duck to water. He in fact became one of the most
proficient and respected domino players on the Island,
entering and even winning tournaments. Today he is a
little rusty, but more than capable of holding his own in any
company. He has always possessed a natural head and
feeling for figures, although his formal education was both
short and restricted. It can be seen now in the speed and
accuracy with which he translates one currency into another.
I remember ordering a large and complicated round in a
foreign bar and asking the barman the cost. I was about to

pay the amount requested when Gary, who fortunately was with me, picked out and corrected the error instinctively before I had time to go to my pocket. Successive West Indian managers have found that, although Gary goes through his salary at great speed, he has always known exactly how much is still due to him. Bookmakers, too, have discovered that Gary can estimate to the last penny what is owed to him, even on the more involved forms of perm betting – 'Yankees', cross-doubles and cross-trebles.

For just over a fortnight Gary learned the strategy of dominoes, and with Dada's help and his own ability became a well-above-average performer in a very short time.

Dada recalls how two experienced players heard that he had a young protégé and challenged Gary and him to a match for money. This was something he could not resist and, although it happened about thirty years ago, he still remembers the details with amusement and pleasure. He and Gary not only won the first encounter, but were even more successful in the return.

Picture the scene, three grown men and a nine-year-old boy battling it out with money at stake. With this beginning it is hardly surprising that Gary became one of the best domino players in Barbados. He would have revelled in Backgammon.

As Gary advanced from child to teenager, to young man, Dada was always there to advise and comfort – the first of Gary's substitute fathers. The relationship began when Gary was six; it still continues.

Although a schoolmaster should never show favouritism, I found, when I was teaching immediately after university, that some children have a special appeal, and it is easy to understand why Everton Barrow was prepared to devote so much of his time to Gary when he went to the Bay Land School.

Everton was young, a good sportsman and an above-average cricketer. It was inevitable that he should become interested in the quiet little boy who had so much ability at ball games. Although his classwork was often sketchy Gary was never troublesome; while on the cricket field, the running track or the soccer pitch he possessed the grace which every sportsmaster longs to see but seldom encounters.

Everton was another who discovered that Gary, though small in size, was old for his years and enjoyed adult company. And Everton, who knew the lad's fatherless background, was able to help in many ways, both in the classroom and on the sports field – Gary being far more appreciative of the latter than the former.

I have already mentioned Briggs Grandison, the groundsman at the Wanderers Club, where Gary and other neighbourhood kids spent so much of their spare time. At first Gary was just another youngster, but Briggs was also a cricketer and quickly realised that this boy had something special. He encouraged him to bowl at the nets and would make suggestions on line and length, where to bowl, change of pace, and flight. A minor father-figure; but the first person to give Gary advice on how to bowl at adult cricketers.

How does one describe Garnett Ashby, the man with whom Gary stayed for those important years playing for Kent Country Cricket Club? Without being sanctimonious I would call him a good man, the type whom one automatically likes because he is kind, full of life and fun (frequently Gary would be taken to matches on the back of Garnett's fearsome motorbike), transparently honest and completely genuine. He immediately appreciated Gary's skill as a cricketer, but also realised that ability without the character to match can be useless. In Gary he found both.

In the beginning Garnett would deliberately leave objects likely to appeal to a small boy of Gary's background lying around his home, as a test of Gary's honesty. To his joy he found that his young protégé had the same standards as he had himself. He came to love the boy as if he were a natural son, not merely because he was brilliant on the cricket field, but for himself.

This was a period in Gary's life when he could easily have gone in the wrong direction and dissipated his talents. He had left school with only a limited education, was very short of money and his future was uncertain. Garnett was the ideal father-figure to have at that time.

Lionel Daniel was younger than most of Gary's early father substitutes, but he, too, did much for him during his formative years. A skilled craftsman who made and sold furniture, he paid Gary pocket money for helping him, although I suspect this was more out of kindness than for any promise in carpentry.

Lionel was a good sportsman and captained the Notre Dame football team, for whom two of Gary's brothers also played. Gary, a very promising schoolboy at inside- or outside-left with plenty of pace and a dynamic left foot – like so many others of his kind – might have developed into another Denis Compton had he been brought up in another environment. When he left school he naturally joined Lionel's club, but his smallness proved a serious handicap on the hard, rough Island pitches.

Like most youngsters with a good pair of hands Gary enjoyed being in goal when players were practising shooting. He was quick, sure and agile and was eventually selected for the Notre Dame XI as goalkeeper. He proved so successful that he was chosen to represent Barbados in this position. This delighted Lionel, but once again it was Gary the person, not merely Gary the sportsman, who attracted him.

That feeling has never died, as I discovered when I walked into Lionel's little factory with the newly-knighted Sobers only a few months ago.

Gary has genuinely always liked people for what they are and has never worried about the colour of their skin. When I asked him if he had ever been embarrassed because of his colour during the many years he spent in England, the only incident he could recall was when he, together with some other West Indian players, was refused admission to a club on his first tour. Even now he is not absolutely sure that colour prejudice was the motive, for he was not wearing a tie at the time! As for the white South Africans who played under him for the World XI, he has never had better support. They gave him respect, loyalty, friendship and one-hundred-per-cent-plus effort both on and off the field.

It is hardly surprising, therefore, that in Police Captain Wilfred Farmer he should have found his first white father-figure. When Wilfred engineered Gary's acceptance for the police band, which enabled him to play senior club cricket for the police, he said he did nothing more than give a boy a chance which he accepted with alacrity. This is much less than the truth, and nobody is firmer on this point than Gary. In addition to improving his cricket, the Barbados police, generally accepted as the most efficient in the West Indies, also gave Gary stability and an understanding of the necessity for law and order in any civilised society. He never showed signs of becoming a tearaway; fights and brawls were not his scene. But the influence of Wilfred and the police ensured they never would be.

His affection for Wilfred was clearly demonstrated when, while staying with me in Essex, he learned by chance that his former captain was ill in a London hospital. Although time was short and he had much to do, Gary was on the first train to London to see him. That, he felt, was the very least he could do for a man who many years before had gone out of his way to help him, for no other reason than that he had realised instinctively the boy had so much to give the world.

John Goddard, who led the West Indies to victory over England in the 1950 tour, was a fine fighting batsman and a useful change bowler. He was captain of Barbados when Gary was first introduced into the side. He was also one of the Island's most influential figures, wealthy and extremely hard-working. He was Gary's first captain in first-class cricket, and was also to take Gary on his first tour. He had seen Gary in action for the police, and had been impressed enough to want him in the Island side despite his youth. An experienced cricketer and shrewd businessman, John kept a fatherly eye on him, having seen too many young coloured players promise much and then, for one reason or another, fall by the wayside. He was determined this should not happen to Sobers. He soon found that Gary was too talented and too committed for this to occur, but he continued to guide and encourage, gaining Gary's respect and confidence, and teaching him much.

John had returned to the West Indies a hero in 1950, but was probably unwise to lead the tour to England seven years later. His team was not so strong, the opposition had improved considerably and he himself was past his peak as a player. The West Indies were heavily defeated in the Tests, and he bore the brunt of the criticism. There is no doubt he and his fellow selectors blundered when they chose the XI for the Lord's Test, but he was over-censured, with the result that he faded from the West Indian cricket scene while he still had much to offer the game.

It was on this unsuccessful 1957 tour to England that Gary began to turn to Everton Weekes, whose background had been similar to Gary's and who had been Gary's hero as a schoolboy. Although knee trouble and a broken finger reduced his run-getting capacity that year, Everton was still recognised as one of the world's foremost batsmen. As a result of his seasons in the Lancashire League he knew English pitches better than most, and in Gary he found an attentive pupil. He also appreciated the dangers of Gary's 'easy come, easy go' attitude to money, and tried to make him a little more careful. It was not easy.

I remember talking to Everton in the 1960s when Gary was bestriding the cricket world like a Colossus. Everton was still having difficulty in making Gary understand the importance of having something put aside for the time when age slowed down that seemingly endless flow of runs and wickets, pointing out that although it was easy for Gary then to increase his standard of living it would be painful having to reduce it later. Gary was initially closer to Everton than to any other senior member of the West Indies side.

The final father-figure was the late Sir Frank Worrell. He exerted considerable influence on every aspect of Gary's later life, and their father and son relationship, or, to be more accurate, elder and younger brother relationship, was to lead to close friendship.

A fellow Barbadian, Frankie had watched Gary develop from a young hopeful in the Police XI to a fully-fledged international, but it was not until the 1957 England tour that the older and more sophisticated man began to appreciate that there was very much more to Gary than a young cricketer of breathtaking possibilities. Sobers, too, was impressed not only by seeing Frankie play one of the most beautifully disciplined innings of his career when he carried his bat for 191 at Trent Bridge after a long spell of bowling, but even more by the way he handled the side when injuries to both captain and vice captain forced him to take over after the final Test. As *Wisden* rightly said at the time: 'Worrell showed unmistakable gifts of leadership.'

Gary's acute cricket brain registered the fact that Frankie was both an astute tactician and a natural leader. He was later to take over from him as professional at Radcliffe, and as they were both living in Lancashire they saw an increasing amount of each other. The friendship ripened and indeed they had much in common. Both were Bajans living in an alien land; both were not only outstanding cricketers but also highly artistic ones; both possessed a tremendous zest for life and both were graceful, handsome men with enormous personal charm.

From Frankie, who had the advantage of a good school and university education, Gary acquired poise, polish and confidence. He also learned much about captaincy, because he toured under Frankie in two memorable tours – those to England and to Australia – which probably did more good for cricket than any in living memory.

Frankie had that positive approach to the game which appealed to the younger man. He also soon discovered that Gary had studied the game deeply and had much to offer on the tactical side. He came to trust his advice and consulted him more and more as time went on. When he decided to relinquish the West Indies captaincy after his last tour of England, Frankie recommended that his protégé, Gary, should inherit his crown. So the prince became king; and immediately demonstrated that, thanks to his apprenticeship, he was ready to take charge.

6

Collie Smith: the Vital Friendship

One Saturday night in 1959 three West Indian cricketers set off for London by car to play in a charity match the next day. Gary was at the wheel. Tom Dewdney, a useful fast bowler, was in the front, with Collie Smith in the back, his eyes closed. A corner, the dazzle of on-coming headlights, a blur, the smash – and a crumpled wreck. It was all over in a matter of seconds. Gary clambered out unhurt. Tom was also lucky. But Collie had to be taken to hospital, where he died shortly afterwards.

His last words to Gary were: 'Go and look after the big fellow, mun.' Tom was in a state of shock and it was typical that, although in great pain himself, Collie's first thought should be for a friend.

After the immediate grief and sorrow had passed the full implications gradually began to dawn on Gary. He had not only lost his best friend, but he had, in effect, killed him. Although it had been an accident, he had been driving and therefore was, to some extent, directly responsible. It was a heavy cross to bear.

It is not easy to describe in words the relationship that grew up between Gary and Collie Smith. In army slang they were 'muckers' or 'mates', the one from the 'littel' wooden house in Barbados and the other from the Boys' Town of Jamaica. They became firm friends when they played together for the West Indies against the Australians in 1954–55, and grew even closer on the tour to New Zealand. By the time they came to England for Gary's first and, alas, Collie's only tour, they were very close. They roomed together, liked the same things, laughed at the same jokes and both had an all-absorbing love for cricket. Gary has always had friends; but Collie Smith was his closest, and his death was to have a considerable impact on Gary's future way of life.

There was never any jealousy, just tremendous mutual admiration and understanding. They knew they possessed exceptional and exciting skills. They had established themselves as regular Test players in their early twenties, and seemed destined for greatness. They recognised and appreciated what each had to offer the game. When they became English League professionals, two young men in a foreign land, they were drawn even more together. They were like brothers. Both benefited from this close-knit friendship which was both tried and true.

I am certain, and so is Gary, that Collie would have become one of the greatest players ever produced by Jamaica and the West Indies. He was a fine, dashing batsman with an exuberant style and the ability to hit the ball with quite astonishing ferocity. I once saw him lose his wicket in a Test match to a catch which went higher than any other I can recall. In addition to his power and the sharpness of his eye, there was a fine temperament and a steadily improving defensive technique. Smith, Sobers and Kanhai were thought of as the natural successors to the three W's and, had he been spared, Collie was as destined for cricketing immortality as a batsman as the other two. However, in addition to this ability and his prowess in the field, Collie was an off-spinner of enormous promise with a teasing flight and a sharp break. Slow bowlers usually take time to reach their peak, and everything suggests he would have become a front-line international spinner. Imagine the difference it would have made to the West Indies – another high-class slow bowler, who would also have been selected purely for his batting prowess. If he had lived, he might conceivably have developed into an all-rounder of a stature which only Gary would have surpassed.

Frank Worrell, at the time captain of the Jamaican XI, had a very high regard for Collie the cricketer, and also for Collie the man. He saw he had the makings of a leader and thought of him in terms of a future captain of the West Indies, and I believe he would have been appointed before Gary – and with Gary's full support. Once again, I would stress the complete harmony and lack of jealousy in each aspect of their friendship.

The two young men found League cricket in England neither as demanding nor as time-consuming as first-class cricket in the West Indies. Both had long leisure periods each week, and yet were earning what was for them very good money. Gary reckons he first became seriously interested in horses and gambling about then. It gave him an interest to fill the vast amount of spare time and prevented him from becoming bored, although it must be admitted that, like so many of his countrymen, he had always fancied a 'flutter'.

It was Collie who provided the stabilising influence. 'Put some of that money you are earning away and send some home. Come on Gary, man, you don't need another drink.' Not that Collie was Puritanical in outlook: quite the reverse. He possessed a zest for life and living which equalled Gary's and a sense of fun which was possibly greater, but he was always conscious of his responsibilities, something he had learned from Father Sherlock of Boys' Town, who had helped him so much in his early days.

The effect of Collie's death on Gary was considerable, and Gary's reaction predictable. He adopted the philosophy of 'eat, drink and be merry, for tomorrow I die' – but substituting 'play cricket' for 'eat'. He was determined to crowd into his own life as much pleasure as possible, for, after all, it was only fate that had decreed he should live and Collie should die. Money became merely something to spend. He gambled more heavily and never contemplated the future because it so easily might never come. Also, for the first time, he began to drink heavily. Until then he had been just a social drinker; now he became an expert performer, who could dispose of a bottle of Scotch or brandy in a session without any trouble. His constitution was remarkable, enabling him to drink through the night and yet play cricket the following morning as if nothing had happened. His natural recklessness, which ironically Collie had been curbing, increased. The days, the nights, were never long enough to allow him to cram everything into them. But he certainly did his best.

In fact he did such a good job that his friends became worried that the excessive pace of his new life-style would have an adverse effect on his cricket. Fortunately for both Gary and West Indian cricket, his avid pursuit of pleasure did not have this effect, because the game provided him with more enjoyment than probably anything else, and his physique enabled him to retain his form despite the considerable strain caused by his extra curricular activities.

Collie Smith had been liked everywhere he went – he was that type of person – so it is hardly surprising to find he was almost idolised in his native Jamaica. Gary was acutely aware of this. It is no coincidence that some of his greatest achievements have been reserved for Sabina Park.

7

The All-Rounders

From the age of three when I first began to play cricket I
have always wanted both to bat and to bowl, a desire which
remained with me throughout my career. I have no regrets
that I became an all-rounder and, indeed, consider myself
fortunate, even though the dual role has certain obvious
snags. The all-rounder cannot hope to score as many runs
as he would if he had concentrated entirely on batting, or
take as many wickets as he would had he specialised in
bowling. He must expect a harder life physically than either
the pure batsman or bowler, especially in the higher echelons
of the game. Thirty overs in a morning and an afternoon can
hardly be regarded as the ideal preparation for a big innings;
while conversely a century is apt to sap the fire of any
opening bowler.

These are not serious problems at school and club level
when most matches are confined to weekends, but it is very
different for those playing six or seven days a week and who
are still expected to provide a good quota of runs and
wickets. In these circumstances it is hardly surprising that
many county cricketers with the ability to become all-
rounders prefer to specialise, becoming either batsmen who
can on occasion take wickets or bowlers capable of making
some runs. Tony Lock of Surrey was a typical example. Had
he been brought up in the West Indies, or Australia, where
there is less first-class cricket, he would surely have been a
genuine all-rounder, rather than a front-line bowler and
useful emergency bat. He could and did play some valuable
innings for England, especially when the going was hard,

but for Surrey he was primarily concerned with his bowling. Runs were largely for fun, bowling for real. The attitude explains England's shortage of all-rounders of international calibre.

However, the advantages of concentrating on both departments more than outweigh the disadvantages. The big attraction to me and, of course, to Gary, was always being in the game. Another bonus was the opportunity of rectifying failure in one department by success in the other. Len Hutton once remarked to me that anything less than a century on his part was apt to be regarded as a failure. The 40 or 50 which would have delighted me were not sufficient for him. In the same way I could be happy with three wickets, whereas Freddy Trueman would be disappointed if he didn't gobble up at least five. The outcome was that I enjoyed my cricket more than most. When I played for Essex solely as a bowler because of a broken finger, or as a batsman because of a torn muscle, it was never as much fun. The total involvement was missing.

Every sport needs balance, and this is what the all-rounder provides in cricket. The ideal team for a Test match should comprise five bowlers, five batsmen and a wicketkeeper. The attack has been put first because this is what wins the majority of matches, apart from those restricted by a given number of overs, or dominated by Bradman-like batting. In most conditions the perfect quintet consists of three seamers, two of whom should be genuinely fast, and two contrasting spinners. There are exceptions. In India, for example, a third spinner, rather than a third seamer, is usually preferable; while on some English wickets, such as Headingley – at least in recent years – two slow bowlers can be superfluous and a fourth seamer an asset.

The weakness of a Test side with five bowlers is that unless some of them or the 'keeper have serious pretensions to batting the team is liable to be short of runs. Two classic

examples of imbalance in Test matches come to mind. In
1949, in the final match against New Zealand, we had –
incredibly – *three* leg spinners – Doug Wright, Eric Hollies
and Freddy Brown; an off-spinner – Jim Laker; three
seamers – Alec Bedser, Bill Edrich and myself; and Denis
Compton as well. It achieved nothing but the expected
draw, and gave us a very fragile batting line-up. The other
occasion was in 1954–55, in the first Test in Australia, when
we chose four pace bowlers – Alec Bedser, Frank Tyson,
Brian Statham and myself. On a good wicket the 'spin
section', consisting of Denis Compton and Bill Edrich (by
then a very occasional bowler), was non-existent. We paid
the price, and lost heavily.

Sometimes the selectors are able to include more run-
getters because one or more of the batsmen are recognised
wicket-takers. To achieve real balance, however, an all-
rounder, and preferably more than one, is essential, because
they can add to the run-potential without reducing the
penetration of the attack.

For them to do this perfectly they should be sufficiently
proficient in both departments to justify their selection in
either capacity. In the lower grades of the game this is
usually quite feasible. I was once asked to captain a Public
Schools representative XI which contained no fewer than
eight recognised all-rounders, an embarrassment of riches
which would have tested the ingenuity of a far more experienced skipper. It was hard enough producing a batting
order that would satisfy everybody, but to employ eight
willing bowlers to the best tactical advantage was impossible.

It is when the selectors come to choosing a Test team,
especially for England, that the difficulty occurs of finding
all-rounders able to measure up to the requirement of
warranting a place in either role. Often the talented county
all-rounder is not quite good enough in either department,
so that there is a tendency to settle for the international

specialist, who can turn his arm over adequately or score some runs if pushed.

It is as an all-rounder that Gary Sobers stands supreme. As a batsman, he would have been an automatic choice for any Test team of any period, and his technique, method and results must give him a place in an all-time world XI. He had the classic pedigree, the ability to destroy an international attack, to rescue an apparently doomed side, to conquer the nearly unplayable pitch and to produce the really big innings, well in excess of a hundred, which is so essential at Test level. He also enjoyed the additional bonus of batting left-handed, and was equally at home against pace or spin.

Gary's second claim to being the greatest and most perfect of all-rounders is based on the fact that he was worth his place in a strong West Indies XI purely as a bowler. Although his bowling never quite acquired the godlike quality of his batting I am inclined to think that in some respects it was even more remarkable, for he is the only person to rank as an international bowler in three entirely different styles. I have never known anyone else adopt three contrasting methods in first-class cricket, let alone in Test matches.

There have been a few who successfully employed two forms of bowling – but never three. Bob Appleyard for a few seasons was able to open the England attack with the new ball before reverting to off-cutters at above average pace which had a very deceiving loop in their trajectory; while more recently Tony Greig has added off-breaks to his repertoire. Bob was an outstanding spinner, but never more than a good seamer. Tony is a slightly unreliable third seamer, and there is still a question-mark against the effectiveness of his off-spin when bowling in England. Another international able to combine seam and spin was the Australian, Bill Johnstone, and a more unusual example of a dual-purpose bowler at the highest level was provided by Yorkshire's Johnny Wardle, who, after years as a very accomplished orthodox slow left-armer, gradually developed into one of the finest wrist-spinners in the world.

To be good enough to bowl in two styles against international batsmen on plumb wickets is hard enough, but to master three is almost uncanny. Without his batting Gary could have earned a place in Test cricket in any of his bowling forms. It is the supreme example of his genius.

The third reason why I rate Gary as indisputably the most accomplished all-rounder in history is that as well as his bowling and batting he was, almost inevitably, a superb all-round fielder. He had the safest of hands, an accurate throw, pace over the ground and very fast reflexes. The versatility which was so noticeable in his batting and bowling applied equally to his fielding. He could field anywhere with distinction, although he is probably best remembered for the effortless way he picked up catches for Lance Gibbs, standing very close at backward short leg, and for his slip catching off the pace bowlers.

Perhaps the best way to appreciate Gary's many talents is to measure them against other outstanding all-rounders. Here, the nearest to Gary must surely be mercurial Keith Miller, exciting, effervescent, brilliant and quite unforgettable. His claims are certainly high. Besides being a magnificent fielder, he would have gained a place in the most powerful Australian XI since the war, and debatably of all time, for either his batting or his bowling. With his partner, Ray Lindwall, Keith formed one of the most feared and effective opening attacks ever. He had a fine, high action which enabled him to obtain lift from even the most placid of pitches, while his bouncer bristled with hostile intent. Although he moved the new ball, one of his most remarkable attributes was the way on a hot afternoon in Adelaide, and the shine long since departed, he could suddenly pitch a delivery on middle and hit the top of the off-stump – to the chagrin and surprise of the recipient.

I would rank Keith purely as a fast bowler ahead of Gary, and definitely nastier with the old ball. In the field there can have been little between them close to the wicket. Keith, when not too involved in the outcome of the next horse race, was probably fractionally ahead in the slips, but at short leg or away from the bat I would place Gary in front. As a batsman Gary was in a different league – sounder, stronger off his back foot and consequently better equipped against pace. He was also far more consistent. There were occasions in England on turning pitches when Keith looked lost; Gary was at his most impressive on such a track. It is only fair to add that he had had far more experience of them because he played the majority of his cricket in England.

The Australian was an exhilarating strokemaster of international class who for various reasons never scored as many runs as his potential warranted. He lacked the discipline to match up to Gary in terms of method and results, and was apt to lose interest. Any captain would dearly love to have either player in his team, but his first choice must be Gary – and I have not even mentioned his other two bowling styles. True, Keith would from time to time slip in a googly to enliven the proceedings, but only for light relief.

Two other outstanding Australian all-rounders deserving consideration are Richie Benaud and Alan Davidson, but here the gap that divides them from Gary is even larger. Richie was a fine leg-break and googly bowler who possessed outstanding control and a tantalising, dipping flight. He was not a big spinner and certainly never turned the ball as much as fellow Australians Bruce Dooland, Cec Pepper and Doug Ring. Relatively speaking, he was more effective overseas than in England, where his haul of wickets was relatively small. Judged purely as a wrist-spinner he was, because of his superior control, better than Gary, but certainly in English conditions the West Indian's seamers constituted

a far greater threat than Richie's leg-breaks. Both were
lithe, athletic fieldsmen. The Australian, however, was never
more than a flamboyant and highly spectacular batsman
capable of savaging the opposition and winning a Test
match, but lacking the defensive technique and run-getting
regularity of a master craftsman. He would probably have
gained his place in several Australian sides simply as an
attacking batsman – but not the Don's of 1948.

A comparison between Alan Davidson and Gary is
especially interesting because both were left-handers, and I
think the Australian might be rated ahead in certainly one,
possibly two, departments. There is a tendency to remember
Alan toward the end of his career, when he was a brilliant
fielder anywhere near the bat and especially round the
corner, where he earned the nickname 'The Claw'. Yet in
the early Fifties when he first appeared for New South
Wales, Alan gained a reputation for running opponents out
through his speed over the ground, combined with the power
and the accuracy of his returns. In those days he was a truly
great outfielder, and I am inclined to place him just ahead
of Gary as an all-purpose fielder. For about five years Alan
was the most feared new ball bowler in the world. He was a
late developer, and on his first two tours of England could
be classified simply as a fine Australian all-rounder. The
change occurred when he added a late swerve to his armoury
of pace and accuracy. Bowling over the wicket, he had the
ability to make the ball dip into a right-hander from the
line of the off stump and just outside it. This forced the
batsman to play at many deliveries which he could have
left alone were it not for the ever-present threat of one dipping
into him. Gary acquired the same ability to swing the ball
into the right-hander from around the area of his off stump,
which was the main reason he claimed the wicket of Geoff
Boycott so many times.

There were other similarities. As new ball bowlers both

had economic run-ups, flowing actions and were of similar speed, but the Australian at his peak, because of the lateness of his swerve, would have been an automatic choice for a world XI simply as an opening bowler. I am not sure that Gary would have made it on that count. On occasions Alan reduced his pace and bowled cutters, but in this style he could never match up to Gary as a spinner. It was as a batsman, however, that he really drops out of the contest. Alan was a dangerous, hard-hitting striker, the ideal person to have coming in about number seven or eight in a Test, capable of caning a wilting attack or leading a rescue act with a spectacular assault. But he was never in the first flight.

Since the war South Africa has produced three distinguished all-rounders, Trevor Goddard, Eddie Barlow and Mike Procter. By combining the talents of all three it might be feasible to match Gary, but not individually. Trevor was a highly competent workman rather than a genius. 'Competitor' sums up Eddie Barlow. He is an effective rather than an attractive opening bat who has outstanding powers of concentration and determination plus an insatiable appetite for runs. His business is batting, and he makes it pay. As a bowler Eddie looks just another seamer, and opponents often pay the price of not treating him seriously enough. He has such fierce faith in his ability that he convinces himself he will succeed, and often does. A perfect example of this occurred in a Cavalier match against Kent. Eddie came on to bowl after Wes Hall, Fred Trueman, Ted Dexter and I had failed to make any impression. In three overs he had not only dismissed both the openers but caused a major collapse. He himself was not even vaguely surprised. He expects to take wickets whatever the circumstances and, of course, he does move the ball a lot. He is also a first-class slip.

Mike Procter measures up closest to Gary because, until injury prevented him bowling seriously, he would have

earned a place in any Test XI both as a fast bowler and as a
punishing, middle-order bat. He was genuinely quick, with
an in-swing of such proportions that he could obtain LBW
decisions from round the wicket. His action was very open-
chested, rather ugly and placed rather too much strain
on his arm and back, but he was both very quick and very
hostile. Unfortunately politics have limited Mike's appearances in Test cricket. Had he been born an Australian he
might well have finished up being rated alongside Keith
Miller – high praise.

Although the West Indies has bred many fine all-rounders
– such as Keith Boyce, Gerry Gomez and Denis Atkinson –
there is nobody who comes in range of Gary. Possibly the
nearest was Sir Frank Worrell, not only another of the
game's immortals but one of the most charming men ever to
have graced cricket. However, to me Frankie will always
remain essentially a great batsman who could bowl effectively,
as distinct from a true all-rounder. Ted Dexter is another in
the same category, while Clive Lloyd is essentially a batsman
who can turn his arm over reasonably well.

John Reid, Vinoo Mankad and Mushtaq Mohammed, of
New Zealand, India and Pakistan respectively, have all
been outstanding all-rounders without seriously challenging
Gary's pride of place. This also applies to the English
contenders. Despite the strain that too much cricket places
on them the counties have still managed to produce some
splendid performers – Brian Close, Ray Illingworth and
Freddy Titmus, for instance. However, none comes within
hailing distance of Gary in terms of international performances and they would be the first to admit the enormous
gulf that exists. The closest to bridging that wide gap must
be England's new captain, Tony Greig, who somewhat
ironically would never have played for England had not
apartheid thrown his native South Africa into the sporting
wilderness.

I saw Tony in the Barbados Test take on the West Indies virtually by himself, capturing six of the eight wickets that fell, catching Sobers full length, left-handed in the slips, and then making more than 150 after the customary collapse at the start of an England innings. Tony certainly commands a place as a batsman in the present Test team. As a dual-purpose bowler he has been more valuable in the Caribbean than in England, but he is steadily improving both as a seamer and as a spinner. He is an asset anywhere in the field, while his obsession with victory and his total involvement mean that he attracts incidents with the inevitability of inflation in the existing economic system. He has also started well in his new role as England captain. Yet, despite his many attributes, he still has a very long way to go.

Inevitably I have asked myself how my own efforts as an all-rounder compare with those of Gary. If I had been able to fulfil my ambitions it might have been close because, as a boy, I wanted to bat like Sir Don Bradman and to bowl like Harold Larwood – not a bad example of 'Man's aim should exceed his grasp, or what's a heaven for?' There was a period when, as a seamer, I might have run Gary close with the ball, but as a batsman it was simply the difference between brass and gold.

What of the giants of the past? Let us take three, Sir Learie Constantine, Frank Woolley and Wally Hammond. I choose them not only because of their proven prowess but because I was lucky enough to have played with all three. Although they were then past their prime, my judgment is not wholly based upon deeds seen through schoolboy-tinted spectacles.

Learie Constantine was the perfect League cricketer, a very fast bowler, a brilliant and frequently unconventional hitter, a fabulous fielder and an inspired entertainer. How he would have revelled in today's limited-overs cricket! It would have been exactly his scene. I was at the other end when I saw Learie *square cut* a ball for six; while as a bowler his beautifully concealed slower ball brought about the end of many batsmen who never picked it and played too soon. Yet his overall performances in Test matches were less convincing, his cost per wicket is high and he did not score all that number of runs. Even if his batting and bowling averages were reversed they still would not come anywhere near those of Gary. Learie is really much closer in style and approach to Keith Boyce, of Essex and the West Indies, who also thrives on one-day cricket.

Of all the batsmen I watched before the war none gave me more pleasure than Kent's Frank Woolley. He must have been close to fifty when I saw him score a half century in about forty minutes off a high-powered Essex attack on a far-from-docile pitch. His sheer elegance was memorable – that and the effortless way he repeatedly lifted the fast bowlers over mid-off with a perfectly straight bat.

I never saw Woolley bowl, but those who did assure me that he was a slow left-armer in the classic mould with a beautiful action and teasing flight. The fact that he completed the 'double' eight times is clear proof he was a top-class bowler, but, unlike Gary, he did not continue as a frontline all-rounder for the whole of his career but instead concentrated on his batting. As a slip he was still, in his fifties, rather better than most and far more graceful. It was this grace as a player that might put Frank ahead of Gary on points, but over the entire span of their batting careers I would take the West Indian to win by a knock-out. If this may sound heretical I suggest a study of their respective records. Gary has been that much more effective.

For unadulterated aptitude Wally Hammond comes nearer to Gary than anyone. In exactly the same way he succeeded at any sport he took up, and after Sir Jack Hobbs is generally agreed to have been the greatest of all English batsmen of his era.

I once had the luck to partner Wally in a stand of over a hundred at Lord's. 'Partner' is probably not quite the right word, as I think my share was about 13, but it did provide me with an absorbing lesson on what batting is all about. To his wonderful skill and the excitement of his performances with the bat must be added his matchless catching in the slips, where, it is said, he held everything without ever deigning to fall over. As a fast-medium bowler with a copy-book action he was also of international class.

The essential difference between Wally and Gary was that the former never chose or attempted to develop his talents as a bowler to the maximum. He preferred to depend upon his batting and was content to be an occasional bowler, albeit a very good one, never completing or bothering about the 'double'. I therefore feel that Wally was not an all-rounder in the full sense of the word, although he obviously could have been had he so desired.

Although they performed their feats in a different world, and so it is impossible to make an accurate comparison of them with Gary, it would be unthinkable to discuss all-rounders without mentioning those two incredible Yorkshire-men Wilfred Rhodes and George Hirst. I met Wilfred on many occasions at Scarborough. He was, alas, blind, but was never happier than when listening to the sound of leather on willow and talking about the game he loved so dearly and had played so well. Eighteen 'doubles' stand for a great many wickets and runs, while he also scored over a thousand runs and took more than a hundred wickets in an age when there was not much international cricket. George Hirst achieved the 'double' sixteen times, and when it is recalled that he bowled around fast-medium pace this represents a considerable physical feat, especially when it is also remembered that in one season he made more than 2000 runs and captured over 200 wickets. This feat never ceases to amaze me. I once experienced the strain of reaching 2000 runs and taking over 100 wickets. To reach 200 wickets I reckon I would have needed at least another three months added to the summer, plus a stretcher to carry me home.

Gary's stamina, on the other hand, is remarkable. On one occasion he joined a Commonwealth team in India straight from Australia. Arriving about midnight after a long and tiring flight he immediately woke up the other West Indian members of the team and as many of the others as he could find and held an impromptu party which went on till dawn.

The four-day match commenced the following morning. On the first day Gary produced some devastating spells of quick bowling, on the second day he played a masterful innings, on the third he turned in another fine bowling performance – this time as a wrist spinner – and on the final day he delighted everybody with a match-winning knock. All his performances were well celebrated the ensuing night, so that Gary had less sleep in five nights than most athletes require in one.

8

The Master Batsman

'I believe Gary Sobers's innings was probably the best ever seen in Australia. The people who saw Sobers have enjoyed one of the historic events of cricket. They were privileged to have such an experience.'

Sir Donald Bradman, of Sobers's 254 for the Rest of the World XI against Australia at Melbourne in 1971

Sir Donald Bradman is generally reckoned to have been the finest batsman, and certainly the most prolific run-getter the world has known. Having in 1948 bowled against him three times, for Essex, for Cambridge University and for the Gentlemen, I endorse this view. Although on that tour the Don was past his peak he scored a century on each occasion, and each one seemed inevitable from the moment he reached double figures. It was a wonderful, chastening experience to watch a genius at work from close quarters. In addition to his legendary feats with the bat the Don was a master tactician, and later became a very distinguished and respected administrator.

When a man of this stature describes an innings in the way the Don did Gary's 254 at Melbourne there can be no finer tribute, especially since the Don has never been extravagant in his praise. It meant the innings was as near perfection as makes no difference.

In their first innings the Rest of the World had been dismissed for 184, with Dennis Lillee taking 5 wickets for 48, including that of Sobers for a duck. In reply Australia reached 285, and the Rest of the World were struggling at

87 for 3 in their second innings when Gary, on a pair, walked to the crease. At close of play three and a half hours later he was 139 not out. When the match was resumed he began carefully before taking his score to 254, which enabled his team to reach 514, even though only one other player, Peter Pollock, reached fifty. Australia managed 317 in their second innings, 96 short of their target. Gary's innings was a classic example of a great knock winning a match.

What appealed to the man who has himself scored over 300 in a day in a Test and averaged a century one out of every three times he strode to the crease was the range and quality of Gary's stroke production, both in attack and defence. In this innings, which contained three sixes and 33 fours, Gary played all the recognised shots (plus a few of his own); the delicate placement, the lofted straight drive against a fast bowler, the square drive off the back foot to both off and leg, the controlled flick off the legs, the imperial hook, and the flowing front foot drive were just some of the delicacies featured in a batting *tour de force*. From start to finish everything was correct: timing, footwork, judgment and execution. They had to be. Nothing less would so have satisfied, captivated and delighted the Don.

Many years earlier Sir Learie Constantine had told Sir Donald to look out for Sobers, a lad who hit the ball harder, and more *consistently* hard than anyone he had encountered. This again was the view not only of an expert but of one who knew far more about hitting than most. Later Bradman was to write in a foreword to *Cricket Advance*:

With his long grip of the bat, his high backlift and free swing, I think, by and large, Gary Sobers consistently hits the ball harder than anyone I can remember. This helps to make him such an exciting player to watch because the emphasis is on power and aggression rather than technique – the latter being the servant, not the master. The uncoiling of those strong, steely wrists, as he flicks the ball

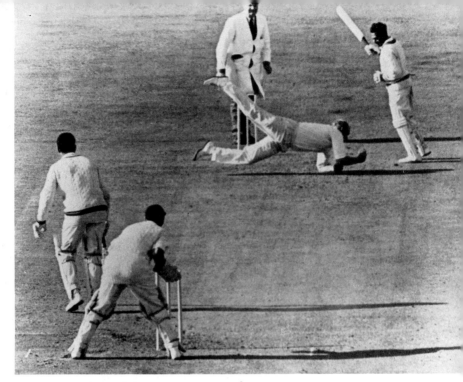

9 Tony Lock makes a brilliant one-handed catch to dismiss Gary for 102 at Leeds in 1963.

10 Returned with interest: Sobers straight-drives Tony Lock for a lofted boundary during the 1968 West Indies game against Western Australia. Gary, unlike the majority of players brought up in bright sunshine, seldom wore a cap.

11 (*above*) Gary and his cousin David Holford leave the field after their famous rescue act for West Indies at Lord's in the second Test in 1966. 12 (*left*) A unique photograph – the only time Gary Sobers was ever unpleasantly hit by a pace bowler in his first-class career. A ball from Richard Jefferson lifts sharply from a length during the MCC and Cambridge University encounter at Lord's in 1961. 13 (*below*) Gary's eldest son, Matthew, watches his father's innings for the Rest of the World v Australia in November 1971.

wide of mid on, is a real joy to watch because it is unique and superbly controlled, whilst the full-blooded square cut is tremendous.

The big hitter in cricket who is also a genuine batsman is like the top-class golfer with a tremendous drive. He excites spectators because he is spectacular, while his power gives him several practical advantages. The golfer's big drive brings him closer to the pin; the batsman's enables him to pierce deep-set defensive fields and greatly increases his chances of getting away with an edged shot. 'If you are going to cut, cut hard' runs the maxim. Then, if the ball finds an edge, there is a reasonable chance it will also clear the slips.

Another asset in being a big hitter is shown when a batsman is attempting a six with fielders out on the boundary. The normal player knows that, unless his timing and execution are perfect, he will probably hole out in the deep, and thus will often opt for a less flamboyant stroke. Gary, on the other hand, knew that if he really middled the ball it would finish up in the stand, or even out of the ground; that even if he failed to make that kind of contact the chances were that it would still carry the field. In other words, he swung so lustily that he could mishit, and still score a six.

How did Gary strike a cricket ball so hard? What was his secret? First, he is tall and well-built, with strong wrists, arms and shoulders. Second, his backlift is both high and straight with a full follow-through. Although one can hit a ball very hard with a short backlift the higher it is the greater the momentum of the bat at moment of impact. Finally, and most important, is Gary's timing: combined with his lovely full swing, build and natural strength, this enabled him to hit out with a destructive force very few have been able to equal. Incidentally, his carry at golf – over 300 yards – is longer than that of many professionals.

Gary's batting philosophy is refreshingly straightforward.

S.G.–F

He considers himself, with every justification, an entertainer, and says quite simply: 'We have got to give the spectator entertainment when we are batting.' This does not mean he despises defence. He knows he has to keep out the good balls, or he cannot score with the consistency required. Therefore his defensive technique is excellent. From his long stay in England Gary has learned to adapt to all types of conditions. However, he has always been an attacking player by nature, seeking to wrest the initiative from the bowler, and is convinced the bat is primarily an offensive rather than a defensive weapon.

At a very early age he realised that bowlers tend to be less effective and menacing if runs are being taken off them and they are seldom beating the bat. What I always found frustrating was when my good ball was dispatched to the boundary by means of a true stroke. I considered the four that resulted from a long hop or half-volley was my fault and was never worried if a perfect delivery was 'hoicked' for four, hoping the batsman would try to take another chance and thus increase the odds of my obtaining his wicket.

The man to fear was the one who scored off a ball of immaculate length without chancing his arm. This was downright disheartening, and was something Gary was able to do more frequently than most. I asked him if he preferred any particular style of bowling; whether he was happier against pace than spin – because most batsmen, even the greatest, are more suspect against one type than another. For instance, Sir Len Hutton was more likely to lose his wicket to an inswinger or an off-break than to a ball leaving the bat; while the reverse applied to Denis Compton. Arthur Morris was wont to have some problems against Alec Bedser's late away swing, and most of the present England side have looked distinctly uncomfortable against real pace.

However, as far as Gary was concerned, once he had established himself at the crease for about twenty minute he did not mind what was bowled at him – pace, swing, seam, spin. He felt capable of dominating them all, and did. He had no physical fear of fast bowling, being so sure of himself that, like Compton before him, he never bothered with a thigh-pad, even against bowlers of the speed of Wes Hall and Dennis Lillee. He argued that he had a bat and that was more than enough protection. Throughout his long first-class career he was hit badly only once, by an unexceptional English fast-medium bowler, when a ball lifted sharply off a length.

Like most West Indian cricketers, Gary was very strong off his legs. He is frankly perplexed when English players deliberately take a ball on their thigh-pad rather than using their bat. This may have stemmed from his early days when a hard ball was used and there were no pads.

Everton Weekes, who was brought up close to the Barbados Test ground, tells how when he was at school two teams of local kids arranged to play a match one Bank Holiday. They clubbed together to buy a composition ball, which Everton, as captain of the home side, took to bed with him, wrapped in cellophane to make it look like the real thing.

The next day, after only a few overs the outer cover of the ball came off. It was not possible to obtain another one, even if they had had sufficient money, because all the shops were shut. But nothing could stop that game. They solved the problem by nailing the cover back on again. This gave them their cricket ball, but with protruding sharp edges of steel. As Everton recalls with feeling, every batsman made absolutely sure he was not hit on the legs that day.

Gary tended to relish the bouncer, aiming to hit it flat and down just behind square if it was travelling through at the right height. He occasionally lost his wicket by mishooking, but over the years it brought him a great many runs. The speed merchants soon became aware that he was not frightened by short fast-pitched deliveries, and that he was inclined to regard them as a welcome invitation to easy runs. Fred Trueman found that bumpers against Gary on a good wicket were an expensive luxury, and seldom bowled them at him, much to Gary's regret.

His method of negotiating the bouncer was simple. If hookable, he used the hook off the back foot; if they were too high he watched them sail by; if they had not risen sufficiently he fended them down off his body with his bat. He always had sufficient time and his footwork was invariably quick and correct. He never ducked, first because it meant taking his eyes off the ball, second because it was never necessary. Wes Hall claims triumphantly that he once forced Gary to duck in Australia – both were representing State teams. Gary says this was an act of courtesy to a great fast bowler, rather than a necessity. I am not going to argue with either version.

Spinners, like all bowlers, usually found bowling against Gary a testing and unrewarding task. Once settled, he refused to let them pin him down and was ever eager and willing to use his feet against them. The wrist spinner probably had more chance than the finger spinner because Gary sometimes failed to pick the googly early on. He recalls that Subhash Gupte troubled him in this way in the West Indies and rates the little Indian leg-spinner as the best he encountered, with Australia's Richie Benaud the most accurate. He also experienced difficulty in reading George Tribe. Like myself, he found picking the googly of the left-hander usually harder than that of the right-hander. Neither of us can understand why. It could be that they are an even rarer breed, but this solution does not really answer the problem.

There was no real flaw in Gary's batting or technique. He was equally at home against all kinds of bowling and was equally happy playing both his attacking and defensive shots off either the front or the back foot. The ideal strategy against him before he was set was to pitch a ball of full length on his off stump and make it hold its own. This should be immediately followed by one of exactly the same line and length, but which then left him fractionally in the air, or, better still, off the wicket. The outcome might well be either a catch behind, or in the slips. If the chance was unaccepted, however, the bowler was liable to regret the lost opportunity for a very long time, as Gary is not the type of batsman who makes many errors.

Although in general it pays to move into line, Gary believes that there are many occasions when it is better to give oneself room to play attacking strokes. This is especially true against quick bowling, when there is little time. As a result he would often force quick bowling without his left foot being in a textbook position. Although the bat might be some way from his body, he could still play through the line with a full, straight swing. This meant there was a risk of his being snapped up behind, if the ball happened to move away, but it also provided him with many spectacular boundaries which delighted spectators and worried the unfortunate bowler.

Gary, when driving off his front foot, would also on occasion deliberately give himself a little extra room by keeping his right leg outside the line, especially when aiming to send the ball square.

What I personally remember and treasure most about Gary's batting are little cameos, moments of magic, in which he showed both his skill and his genius, like the shot he played off Tony Buss on a sodden pitch at Hove in a Cavalier match. Tony, who has a good leg cutter, pitched this to Gary perfectly. It turned, stopped and lifted. It was a ball most batsmen would have been proud simply to play safely, but Gary went on to his back foot and drove it on the up along the carpet to the boundary with an absolutely straight bat. I can still see every detail as plainly as when I watched it with my mouth open from the other end.

Then there was the time when I was captaining the Cavaliers in Jamaica and Gary completed a beautiful century in the grand manner. He went down the wicket to a good ball from Robin Hobbs and effortlessly drove it over extra cover into the crowd.

I remember bowling to him in a Test during the West Indies tour of England in 1957. He was still in the apprentice stage, and I was certain I had found the 'gate' with a delivery pitching off-stump and coming back really sharply. Just when it seemed the ball was through Gary adjusted so that he not only kept it out of his stumps, but did it with the middle of his bat.

All batsmen experience a bad patch from time to time and Gary was no exception, but what he did not like about his lean spell in Pakistan, which followed his Indian fiesta of 1958–59, was that it stemmed from the umpiring and not his own batting.

Before the first Test in Pakistan his manager, Berkeley Gaskin, warned Gary that he would not score many runs. Gary said: 'I could not understand why at the time, as I had just made over a thousand in India. But I soon found out.

'In the first innings I was forcing the ball to leg and was struck on the outside of the right leg – and was given out LBW. I was amazed, but just put it down as one of those things. I discovered it was rather more than that when I was LBW'd out in the second innings as well.'

At Dacca in the following Test Gary was on the receiving end of his third consecutive LBW and was firmly convinced there was a deliberate plot to stop him making runs. He was so incensed he saw no point in remaining and wanted to return home, but was talked out of it by the sensible and sympathetic Gaskin.

There are many players who believe they are never out and that it is always an umpiring mistake. Gary is not one of these. He has exceptional judgment of where the ball pitches, he plays very straight and he does not employ his pads as a second line of defence, as, for instance, even so good a batsman as Colin Cowdrey does. He relies upon his bat both in attack and defence, and accepts umpiring decisions rather better than most. I would put him very high on my list of honest batsmen, which is borne out by his attitude to 'walking', about which he has this to say:

'I walk because, when you know you have hit the ball, I believe it is cheating if you don't. The umpires have a very difficult job to do and should be helped as much as possible, and this is one way.

'Some people think it is the umpire's job to judge them, but I can't stay there and wait for a decision if I know I have hit it.'

This may all sound too good to be true, but those who have played with Gary know that he adhered to this philosophy. On the other hand, he had the sense never to try to enforce his views on other players – it must always be a personal decision.

I also favour batsmen walking, at least in theory. Although umpires should not be influenced by the actions of the players, they are human and *are* influenced. To an extent they get to know the walkers and non-walkers, with the result that a batsman with a reputation for always walking will sometimes take advantage of this by failing to do so when the chips are down. It is on these occasions I have doubts and wonder whether it is not wiser to leave it, Aussie fashion, entirely to the umpires without deliberately assisting them. This has the advantage of lessening ill-feeling against a batsman after a questionable decision, because the fielding side can hardly blame him for abiding by a recognised code.

As it was, a sadly disillusioned Sobers completed the

Pakistan tour. He hit an excellent 70 in the final Test, but the fun had gone. He drank more than usual as a relief and a refuge.

Of all the countries Gary has played Test cricket against, he has been least successful with the bat against New Zealand. This is surprising as they are certainly not the most powerful. He has no excuses. His big disappointment is that the New Zealand crowds have never had the opportunity of seeing him in full flow. It is difficult to explain.

Certainly the pitches in New Zealand tend to assist the bowlers, but Gary's technique enables him to cope with these far better than most. I have an idea one of the reasons, and without being disrespectful to New Zealand attacks, or their cricket, is that they have been a side the West Indies always expected to beat and that this caused Gary, quite unintentionally, to relax a little.

It is easy to give one's wicket away, but it takes an artist to do this as well as Gary did to me in a Benefit game in the Sixties. He decided he had provided sufficient entertainment and had scored enough runs, so he got out. Nothing unusual about that. It was the way he did it which typified both the man and his craft. He waited until I sent down a ball of good length which pitched on his leg stump and hit the middle as he played a full forward defensive stroke, deliberately and fractionally down the wrong line. He made it look a very good delivery – it wasn't a bad one! But he played his shot so well that the wicket-keeper and first slip – though both county professionals – came up to congratulate me. I knew instinctively what Gary had done. But no spectator realised it was an act of charity; only Gary and myself.

9
Some Outstanding Innings

Many of the game's great players have been – and are – very record-conscious. They have always sought records avidly, and the pursuit of runs for runs' sake has been a driving force. They have a memory for their own scores and a great concern about having their name in the record books, while they tend to forget why the runs were needed. This has never applied to Gary, who has acquired more records than most. These were only incidentals, never prime objectives. He made his runs because they were necessary to win matches, not because they supplied him with another century. The outcome is that he must rate, along with Denis Compton, who had exactly the same approach, as one of the most unselfish of batsmen. He always put the needs of his side first and in so doing frequently sacrificed his wicket without thinking about it. In fact, Gary has considerable difficulty in remembering even some of his finest performances.

It took him a long time to decide what he thought was the most outstanding innings of his career. He finally settled for the Lord's Test against England in 1966.

The West Indies had been bowled out in their first innings for 269, the English seam quartet of Higgs, Jones, Knight and D'Oliveira claiming all the wickets in conditions which favoured this form of attack, as is so often the case at Lord's on the opening day of a match. England replied with 355, and then their seamers struck again. The tourists, with five wickets down, a lead of 9 runs, and the ball moving about, seemed destined for a heavy defeat. It was then that Gary was joined by his cousin, David Holford. Against all the odds this pair proceeded to put on 274 runs for the fifth wicket, which enabled them to declare at 369 for 5, with Sobers 163 not out and Holford 105 not out.

Sobers and Holford's remarkable partnership was more than a determined rearguard action. Both master and pupil gathered their runs sufficiently fast to allow Gary to declare, and although the game eventually ended in a draw Gary demonstrated yet again his belief in positive cricket, whereas most captains would have concentrated on trying to save the game.

Gary confessed he thought all was lost when Holford came to the wicket. 'At 95 for 5 we were in real trouble. Colin Cowdrey was setting a very attacking field, so I decided to attack to make him remove some of his close fielders.'

This tactic proved so successful that Gary eventually regained the initiative. Throughout the record-breaking stand he deliberately did not try to shield his partner by taking most of the strike. He believed, correctly, that if he himself batted really well his presence would inspire Holford to produce the innings of his life. He showed his cousin that the English bowlers could not only be played, but also punished – and the message registered. They not only saved the game but might even have snatched an impossible victory, had not Colin Milburn came to England's rescue with a fine century in their second innings.

In general, Gary believes in allowing his partners to stand on their own feet, rather than attempting to monopolise the bowling by pinching a single off the fifth or sixth ball of each over. If he showed the way then the more bowling the other player received the more confident he would become. On that occasion, and many others, this approach worked. It certainly made batting easier if one had Gary Sobers at the other end.

What pleased him especially about that come-back at Lord's was that it showed that the West Indies had the determination and character to climb off the floor when all seemed lost. Up to that match there was a tendency to say that they batted well when on top, but lacked the resilience of Australian and English teams who have so often fought their way back into a game.

For the next outstanding innings one needs to go back a bit. Gary on his first tour to England had impressed everyone with his batting potential, but he had not scored a Test century. Attractive fifties and sixties are fine up to a point, but it is the big individual innings that win internationals, and great batsmen produce them with regularity. He realised that if he were to achieve his ambition of equalling and eventually surpassing the deeds of the great Three W's he would soon have to start registering three-figure scores in Tests.

By the time Pakistan came on a tour of the West Indies in 1958 most people felt a Sobers Test hundred was in the offing, but nobody expected his first major innings would also turn out to be the highest ever recorded in international cricket.

This remarkable score was made in the West Indian first innings in the very first Test. When they went in to bat the West Indies faced a total of 328. Gary, sent in to open the innings, first mastered the Pakistan attack and then proceeded to destroy it on a good, fast Sabina Park wicket. He received splendid support from Conrad Hunte in a massive second wicket stand of 446. Eventually, when Hunte had scored 260, he was run out – the only way either appeared likely to go. But Gary simply continued with the insatiable appetite of a youngster for more and more runs, until Sir Len Hutton's record Test score came into sight.

Gary admits how lucky he was to have the experienced

Clyde Walcott with him at this juncture. Clyde knew exactly
what making the highest-ever Test score would mean to a
young professional cricketer. He went down the wicket to
Gary and said just the right words. 'You get the runs and
I'll keep you going.'

With this encouragement Gary took his score to 365
not out, at which point the innings was declared closed at
790 for 3. This proved too much for the 20,000 spectators,
who in their elation and excitement invaded the ground and
damaged the pitch. This meant that play was abandoned
for the day and the West Indian captain was unable to
pick up some wickets in that final hour, when the opposition
could only have been extremely tired and dispirited. As
things turned out this did not matter, as Pakistan were
bowled out for the second time in the match with nearly a
day to spare, and lost by the considerable margin of an
innings and 174 runs.

Gary does not consider this his most important innings.
For one thing, the Pakistani attack was rather threadbare.
Kardar, the Pakistan captain, went into the match against
doctor's advice with a broken finger on his spinning hand,
but sent down 37 overs; Mahmood Hussain pulled a muscle
in the opening over and took no further part in the proceedings; while Nasim-ul-Ghani was put out of action early
on with a fractured finger. This placed an immense burden
on Fazal Mahmood and Khan Mohammad. Even so, 365
runs still constitute a remarkable feat of endurance, skill
and concentration. It is also worth mentioning that Gary
batted for only just over ten hours and never stopped playing
strokes. This was more than three hours quicker than Hutton
had taken at the Oval, nineteen years previously against
Australia – and which had also been accomplished against
a less than full-strength attack. The innings established Gary
as one of the outstanding batsmen of all time. It was an
inspiration, because he had reached the very top in the game

and from then on never looked back. Cricket-lovers everywhere wanted to see him bat. He had hit the big time.

Another of Gary's memorable innings at Sabina Park was
against England in 1968. It was a further notable rescue-act
against the odds, which this time were increased by a very
untrustworthy pitch. The West Indies had been shot out
in their first innings for well under two hundred and Gary
himself had failed to trouble the scorers. Despite a brave
innings by Seymour Nurse his side had to follow on, and
were close to defeat when Gary came in at Number 6.

On that unpredictable wicket a batsman needed some
luck to survive and Gary was put down in the slips early on,
but only a cricket genius could have hoped to score a not out
century – his final score was 113 – and inspire his colleagues
at the other end. He was eventually able to declare at 391
for 9 and his team came very close to snatching what would
have been a miraculous win from sure defeat. England,
68 for 8 at close of play in their second innings, were in
deep trouble against the spin of Gibbs and Sobers. Gary
himself ended with bowling figures of 3 for 33.

In terms of the situation and the vagaries of the pitch this
was undoubtedly one of Gary's finest performances with the
bat. Inevitably he played more false strokes than such a
perfectionist likes to do. He was forced to improvise, stabbing
out the shooter and taking the occasional calculated risk
so that the bowlers were never permitted to dominate to the
extent that they should have done. He admits he enjoyed a
lot of luck. I wonder just how much he made for himself by
his own ability.

On his first tour to Australia in 1960–61 under Sir Frank
Worrell, Gary, after a good start, experienced a lean spell
which was also reflected in his team's performances. The
culmination was a heavy defeat by New South Wales, in

which he made 2 and 0. He recalls sitting in the dressing room thinking about the runs that were not coming when Richie Benaud came in and the Australian team manager introduced them with the words: 'Don't you worry, son. You'll get to pick him some time.'

Gary, who had had trouble in reaching Richie's googly, was not exactly bursting with confidence when shortly afterwards the West Indies met Australia, captained by Benaud, at Brisbane in the first Test. He cast aside his doubts to hit 132 runs in 123 minutes in a breathtaking exhibition of attacking batsmanship which set the tone for the series and caught the imagination of the cricketing world. All the Australian bowlers suffered, not least Richie Benaud.

What pleased Gary so much about that particular knock was the fact it came at the perfect psychological moment. The Australian critics had not thought much of the West Indian chances before the Test, and indeed when Gary came to the crease they were already 42 for 2 – soon to be 65 for 3 – with Alan Davidson in full cry. With Frank Worrell (later to describe Gary's innings as the best he had ever seen him play) stabilising at the other end, Gary mounted a blistering counter-attack which brought up the hundred partnership in ninety minutes and set the game alight. Runs came at such a pace – despite some deep-set field placings by Benaud – that the new ball, available after 200 runs, was taken at only 25 minutes past two on the *opening day* of a Test.

Of the whole innings that excellent cricket-writer, Jack Fingleton, wrote in *Fingleton on Cricket*:

'It is not easy to decide which innings is the greatest one has seen. In the circumstances, one would give the accolade to McCabe's in 1932, yet I consider myself fortunate to have seen this one by Sobers.'

One of the people lucky enough to see Gary's *tour de force* in Brisbane was Sir Donald Bradman. He was excited by both the method and the execution, which must have reminded him in some ways of his own youth. He began to think what it could mean to Australians if he could bring Gary back to take part in their domestic cricket, and he did so successfully.

Gary has great respect and affection for the Don and I am by no means sure that his comment immediately after that innings in the first Test did not give him as much satisfaction as the innings itself. Said the Don sardonically: 'Thank you very much, son, I knew you wouldn't let me down, and it's a good thing that you could not pick Richie, or you would have murdered him!'

Gary naturally found the perfect Indian wickets much to his liking. In the 1958–59 tour out there he underlined this point with three successive centuries. The one that gave him most satisfaction was 142 not out at Bombay, because he was suffering from a very bad back, the result of a spinal injection for appendicectomy. He was in considerable pain throughout the innings, and eventually collapsed at the crease and was taken to hospital. Here he was given another injection in the affected part without a sedative – which proved to be even more unpleasant than the back had been when batting. However, it did the trick. Or possibly Gary decided not to have any more injections.

There are many examples of Gary's prowess as a big hitter, including lofting Alan Davidson with the new ball over the straight scoreboard at Adelaide, an enormous blow by any standards. But the most remarkable was that record-breaking over for Notts against Glamorgan at Swansea in 1966 when he smote the helpless Malcolm Nash for six sixes in one over, the first and only time this has been accomplished in the history of first-class cricket.

It was not a carefully planned assault on a world record, as Roger Bannister's had been when he broke the four-minute barrier for the mile. It owed nothing to intentional co-operation from opponents, as did that hurricane hundred by Robin Hobbs against the Australians at Chelmsford in 1975. Gary's six sixes simply occurred in the context of the game, and it was not until he had hit four of them that thoughts of making a new record even entered his mind.

With more than 300 for 5 on the board in their first innings Gary wanted quick runs for a declaration. Nash, one of the established Glamorgan bowlers, was bowling steady left-arm spinners. He was just beginning to develop this style of attack, having originally been a swing and seam bowler. Gary simply hit each ball on the rise into various sections of the delighted crowd, who had never seen such a burst of controlled hitting before and are never likely to see it again.

The first three deliveries were despatched high over mid-on, mid-wicket and mid-off. The fourth ball was pulled over square leg. Gary struck the fifth too far up his bat, near the splice, and was caught by a fielder right on the boundary. Typically, he was already walking back to the pavilion when he was recalled by the umpire. The fieldsman had carried the ball over the boundary line, much to the relief of the enthralled spectators.

It was not until his fourth consecutive six, all off good-length balls, that Gary thought in terms of an over of sixes and decided to go for the lot. The crowd was really buzzing with expectancy, and Wilf Wooller, who was commentating for television, was almost hysterical with excitement. Nash's final ball was a deliberate seamer, but he made the mistake of digging it in too short; it was last seen hurtling into the outskirts of Swansea.

Peter Walker, fielding at slip at the start of this remarkable over and thankful his stint of bowling was from the other end, summed up that last mighty blow: 'It wasn't a six. It was a twelve!'

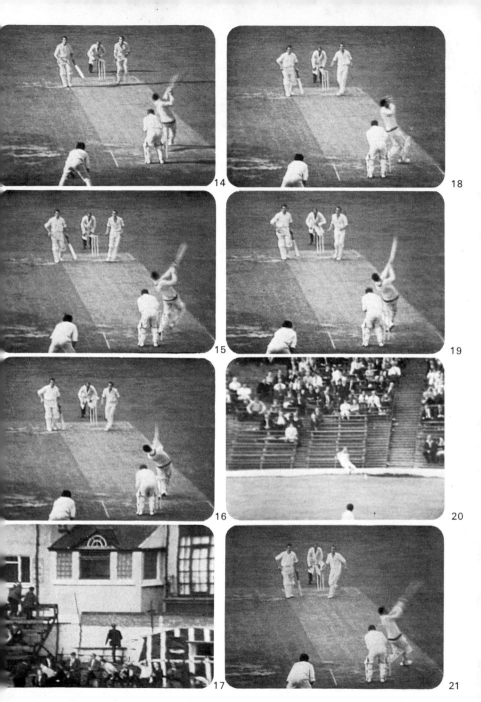

Operation Over-kill

Gary's record six sixes in an over v Glamorgan in 1968. **14** Ball One – Away she goes.
15 Ball Two – Still further ! **16** Ball Three – The straight drive. **17** The Members Stand
under bombardment. **18** Ball Four – The pull. **19** Ball Five – Not quite middled.
20 Caught, but not out. **21** Ball Six – The record achieved.

22 In the leg trap : the famous catch at Old Trafford in 1966 to dismiss Eric Russell for 26 during the England first innings. 'Ct Sobers b Gibbs' was to be an oft-repeated double act.

23 A spectacular attempt to catch Ken Barrington during the second Test Match at Leeds the same year. Despite Gary's efforts the ball went through for four.

10

The Triple-Purpose Bowler

Gary is one of that small, select band who have captured more than 200 wickets in Test cricket. By itself, this would ensure him a place in the game's history, but in his case it was accomplished by using three entirely different styles of bowling – seam, orthodox finger-spin and wrist-spin. I personally find this unique ability to combine three contrasting forms of attack even more remarkable than his skill as a batsman. Although Gary was, in every respect, a superb strokemaker, there have, over the years, been rivals. But there has never been a more complete bowler at international level, nor probably at any level.

Gary's bowling average in Tests was 33, which may well appear expensive. Why was it so high? There are several pertinent reasons. First, he was essentially an attacking bowler in method and inclination. His main consideration was getting the batsmen out rather than keeping them quiet. This was especially true of his roles as wrist-spinner and new-ball operator.

Second, a considerable portion of his international series were in the Caribbean, where the pitches are usually far more sympathetic to batting than to bowling. Although English Test wickets can be real featherbeds, like the one at the Oval in 1975, when six days were not sufficient to produce a result, the weather or the atmosphere comes to the aid of the bowlers far more frequently than they do in the West Indies. Also, in England the pitches are left uncovered during the hours of play, which again helps the bowler.

Third, toward the end of his career, Gary was part of an attack which lacked penetration; some bowlers were on the wane, while the newcomers were often not up to standard. This reduced his own effectiveness and meant that he had to bowl too much and in conditions which were far from helpful.

Finally, in the days when Wes Hall and Charlie Griffith were causing havoc with their pace and Lance Gibbs was the front-line spinner Gary was main support to all three. He was the person who had to come on up the hill and into the wind, while, if the ball was turning at all, he would usually have second choice of ends. Even so, it is my belief that if he had not used up a certain amount of effort in scoring more runs than anybody else, he must surely have broken the record for the number of wickets taken.

There is no detailed breakdown of the three different methods Gary used and their wicket-taking effectiveness. To be realistic, this could never have been done, because at his peak Gary was always switching styles.

Of his three methods, it was as a fast, seam and swerve bowler that he was most feared, even though he did not start to bowl this style seriously until he had established himself in Test cricket, first as an orthodox slow left-armer and then as a batsman.

He developed into a seamer while playing in English League cricket. On many of these pitches pace was more likely to succeed than left-arm finger-spin. Gary recalls he had always possessed the ability to send down a fast delivery. This had proved a big advantage in those early days of beach and street games – especially when the ball was hard and the batsman was not wearing pads!

His speed derived from a beautiful body action – classically perfect, head looking over the outside of a high right arm, left arm completing a full arc before chasing the right across his body in a full follow-through. It derived, too, from his timing, in that he released the ball at exactly the right moment after he had landed on a braced right leg. In the nets he found that he could bowl quicker off a shorter run than most recognised seamers. It was not long before he was causing greater problems as a pace bowler than he had as a spinner. Initially his success stemmed from his speed, line and length. The subtleties of swing and seam were to come later, but a lively left-armer from over the wicket is always liable to cause trouble because of the pronounced difference in line. Batsmen become so accustomed to playing the ball from the right-arm, over-the-wicket bowler, with the ball pitching outside the off-stump, that they are inclined to do exactly the same to a left-arm, over-the-wicket delivery which it would often be better and safer to leave alone.

When Frank Worrell took over the captaincy of the West Indies he immediately realised how much more formidable his team would become were Gary able to take on the additional role of third seamer. Frankie had himself been a very useful, lively medium-pace swing bowler as well as an occasional spinner, so that he was well qualified to appreciate the new dimension which Gary provided by his pace and ability to move the ball. But although he bowled some seam in India it was not until the 1960–61 Australian Tour that Gary came to be regarded as a quick bowler of truly Test-calibre.

One advantage of Gary developing so late as a 'quickie' was that he did not risk burning himself out in his youth before he had fully matured physically. A seventeen- or eighteen-year-old with aspirations for speed is unlikely to settle for that short, controlled twelve-pace run-up which was all that Gary required. He will probably try something much more spectacular, even though it takes a lot out of him and has less rhythm.

How quick was Gary? It is difficult to judge; on his first tour of Australia he was often distinctly quick, but in his later years, after the second knee operation, his speed dropped to around fast-medium.

Gary reckons that, when he really chose to slip himself, which he did from time to time, he could send down the odd delivery that was just as fast as anything from Wes Hall, or a Charlie Griffith's yorker. However, speed was not Gary's chief weapon. What worried the good players was his ability to dip the ball back into the right-hander and make the odd one move away off the pitch. He could achieve more swerve than either Wes or Charlie, which was one reason why he sometimes opened with the new ball if conditions favoured swing. He did this to good effect, for instance, in the second innings of the Leeds Test of 1963. England, who required an improbable 453 to win, began badly with Gary striking in his first over and going on to pick up three out of the first four wickets.

Over the years he managed to trap Boycott with the new ball several times just because of this ability to move the ball late. Once he deliberately put himself on to open the bowling against England at Trent Bridge, and trapped Boycott for o with his in-dipper, having estimated that the Yorkshireman's technique made him slightly vulnerable to this delivery at the start of an innings. This did not mean that Boycott failed to score runs against the West Indies – quite the reverse; but Gary always fancied his chances against him with a 'new cherry'.

Another reason for Gary opening the attack was to save time. His short run-up meant that he was able to send down more overs. This was especially useful during that difficult last sixty or thirty minutes when the opposing opening bats were struggling to stay until the close.

Although he could unleash a vicious bouncer, all the nastier because of its rarity, Gary was essentially an attacking seamer who believed in keeping the ball up to the bat. He wanted batsmen to attempt to force him. They might drive him for four, but if he was able to move one it might induce a false stroke. He could on occasion bowl tightly and defensively, but this was never his scene. His prime objective was ever to get the opposition out, rather than to stop them scoring.

Gary's career as a chinaman and googly bowler was short. He bowled it seriously for less than five years, so we shall never know just how good he might have become had he practised longer this most demanding of all styles. However, in that brief period he mastered the very difficult art well enough to take wickets regularly both in Test and Australian State cricket. Only class wrist-spinners are capable of this.

It began, rather like his seam bowling, while he was playing in the Lancashire League. Gary had always been able to spin the ball more than most, as his opponents at Little Cricket, back in his childhood, still testify. Because he had an enquiring mind he liked to experiment. It was therefore only natural that he should send down a chinaman – a left-hander's leg-break which is an off-break to a right-handed batsman – in the nets from time to time. He was quick to note the almost hypnotic effect the mere sight of a wrist-spinner has on a high percentage of quite reasonable club cricketers. The outcome was that he would produce the odd chinaman in a match and, as he was often rewarded with a wicket, he began to bowl them more often.

Although it is possible to obtain wickets at club level merely by sending down chinamen, in first-class cricket the bowler must also be able to disguise his googly, otherwise any good right-hander will systematically destroy him. Gary quickly appreciated this and immediately set out to produce a googly that would be difficult to pick, that would turn and, most important of all, that he could pitch. As with everything connected with the game, it came more easily and faster to him than to others. There are many who maintain that it takes ten years for a leg-break and googly bowler to learn his trade, but Gary was bowling this style well enough to worry first-class batsmen in less than two seasons!

Wrist-spin bowling appealed to Gary for many reasons. First, it represented a new art to master. Second, it is essentially an attacking form of bowling. The wrist-spinner's main objective is to dismiss batsmen, not to keep them quiet. He cannot hope to possess as much control as the finger-spinner, but he can turn the ball on perfect pitches when the latter may fail to 'bite'. Third, wrist-spin breaks are far more satisfying to bowl than seam-up, or finger-spin, which is why so many front-line batsmen dabble in them – Cowdrey, Barrington, Hutton, Fletcher and Graveney, to name but a few. They are fun and there can be few greater delights in the game than bowling a batsman with a googly which he is cutting because he is under the impression that it is a leg-break.

Gary's life as a front-line wrist-spinner ended in 1966 when his shoulder went as a result of bowling the googly. It never completely healed. This is by no means an uncommon happening to spinners who bowl googlies with a high arm action, as it does put a considerable strain on the shoulder. Had he been a right-arm bowler, the loss of his googly would not have been so serious, for there have been many successful leg-break bowlers without a googly who rely on the leg-break and the top-spinner alone. Gary could still bowl his chinaman, but that, without a googly to back it up, would never seriously inconvenience top-class players, who can hit happily with the spin.

The wrist-spinner needs plenty of bowling in the middle, plus practice. He must be prepared to accept rather more punishment than other types, because he is unlikely to be quite as accurate, while an ultra-slow pitch can be death to him. Neither of these facts worried Gary, since he has, as I have mentioned, never been concerned about cost, or average-conscious. His main handicap was that he simply did not have the opportunity to do sufficient wrist-spin bowling, concentrating on nothing else.

Before going on to bowl spin, he would, more often than not, have had a considerable spell with the new ball. Then again, on a pitch which was proving too slow for him, but suited Lance Gibbs, he would probably revert to finger-spin. It followed that he was relatively more effective as a wrist-spinner on the quicker pitches in Australia than in England where they are becoming an extinct species.

Although Gary began as an orthodox slow left-armer, was good enough to take wickets in Test cricket as one, and bowled them intermittently throughout his career, it was certainly his least exciting style and the least impressive. One of the best examples of his causing trouble as an orthodox left-armer occurred as recently as his last tour to Australia. He employed this method in the Australian second innings at Brisbane, after a few perfunctory overs with the new ball. His 6 wickets for 73 in a very long spell was largely responsible for that West Indian victory.

If you were to go up to Gary and say he had made so-and-so runs, or taken so many wickets on such-and-such an occasion, the odds are that he would say, 'Oh, did I?' He does not remember, with certain obvious exceptions, his individual records, recalling the incidents and the incidentals relating to the performance rather than the performance itself. I asked him, off-the-cuff, to pick out one particular bowling feat. There was a considerable delay and then he said 'Oh, mun, I was tired at Melbourne. I bowled some thirty eight-ball overs, picked up a few wickets, kept going non-stop for nearly five hours and came off the field absolutely dead, but very satisfied.'

This marathon bowling feat occurred in the Australian first innings of the Fifth Test in 1961. Gary had gone on with the score 124 for 0 and did not come off until it was 335 for 9. In the process he took the second new ball and his final figures were 44–7–120–5, a magnificent spell of bowling in one of the truly historic Tests, which Australia just won by two wickets.

Another piece of bowling which gave Gary particular satisfaction was in the first innings of the opening Test between England and the Rest of the World at Lord's in 1970, one of his favourite grounds. On a cloudy day he came on first change and, moving the ball all over the place, sent his opponents reeling to what was to be an overwhelming defeat. They were all out for 127, and Gary finished with 6 for 21: at one stage he had 6 for 11. This was his most devastating spell in international cricket, which he followed up with an innings of 183 and a couple more wickets when England went into bat again. It is, of course, one of the most remarkable all-round efforts ever achieved at this level.

Gary's attitude to bowling was, like his batting, essentially positive. Whatever the style, he hustled through his overs. He worked on the theory that the more balls he could send down in a given period the greater the chance he had of securing wickets. He never approved of the deliberate slowing-down of over rates so often practised by English teams, especially overseas. A three- or four-minute over for slow bowlers with short run-ups, he reckoned, offends the spirit of cricket.

When Gary was playing for South Australia against the South Africans in 1963 Sir Donald Bradman called him 'the five-in-one cricketer'. Later Gary was to become a 'six-in-one cricketer', when to his other five roles was added the role of captaincy. If anyone still doubts that Gary was the ultimate all-rounder this new role and the extra burden involved must surely convince him.

11
Captaincy

To be a successful cricket captain, or football manager, the first requirement is to have good players. The most accomplished captain cannot win matches without them. He can improve a bad side or make a good side better, while there are a few captains, and rather more managers, who can be guaranteed to ruin any team. However, at cricket, in the main, given knowledgable, intelligent players, a well-balanced attack and a good batting line-up any side is bound to do well. It is not difficult to govern a powerful XI; what is difficult is captaining a poor one on the decline. Both Sir Donald Bradman and Sir Len Hutton were fine skippers, but it would not have required a tactical genius in charge for Australia to have captured the Ashes in 1948, or for England to have won them in 1956.

In England there is a tendency to exaggerate the importance of leadership and team spirit. Two of the most successful English captains, Hutton and Illingworth, have been astute tacticians rather than great leaders, while the two strongest attacks I have encountered in county cricket consisted of bowlers, who, far from working in harmony, actively disliked one another.

When Sir Frank Worrell decided to retire from the international game after a memorable spell as skipper, he recommended that Gary should take over, rather than Conrad Hunte, who had been his vice-captain. His reasoning was logical enough. Gary was the finest cricketer in the world, he was younger than Conrad, the responsibility would tone down his *joie de vivre* and Conrad's religious convictions might unintentionally have embarrassed some of the men playing under him.

When offered the West Indian captaincy in 1965 Gary was distinctly apprehensive. He was flattered, but by no means sure he wanted the job – or sure that ne was, at that stage, right for it. He was so wrapped up in simply playing the game that he was worried leadership might prove to be a handicap. After receiving the invitation from the West Indian Board, which he half expected, he took nearly a month to reply, not, for once, because he was dilatory, but because he could not make up his mind. His own fears that it might affect his play were shared by many West Indians. On the other hand, he did have one big advantage, the practical experience he had acquired as Worrell's right-hand man and unofficial first lieutenant. Frankie had frequently discussed moves and tactics with him, off as well as on the field, and their thinking was often identical.

The ideal time to take over a team is in many respects when it is doing badly. Then whatever happens must almost inevitably be an improvement. The odds were always strongly against Sir Matt Busby's successor at Manchester United, for instance. If the club did well it was only to be expected. If it started to slip it was largely the new manager's fault. He was on a loser to nothing.

Gary suffered from taking over from Worrell, who is generally considered to be the greatest of all West Indian captains. As a result he never quite received the credit he deserved for winning his first three series, even though he was short of experience. Under him the West Indies beat Australia, for the first time ever, England and then India. This was a tremendous start by any standards and quickly silenced the early doubters. Had Gary retired at that juncture he would have gone down as the most successful of all Caribbean skippers.

Only in the Australian series were there any signs that the

added burden would lessen his contribution as a player. In ten innings his highest score was only 69 and his twelve wickets were costly. This is what *Wisden* said about him despite his unimpressive figures in the Rubber:

'He was three great players in one, and he seemed to thrive on his extra responsibilities of leadership. As a captain he showed an instinctive tactical sense which never let him down. He was a worthy successor to Sir Frank Worrell. No higher praise can be given.'

This appreciation of his first efforts as captain refutes the views of those who have questioned his ability as a captain in his later, and less successful, period. Skippers may lose some of their enthusiasm, and I agree with Ian Chappell that it is possible to captain an international XI for too long. But tactical appreciation should, like wine, improve with the years.

After those three triumphant series came a long list of disappointments as captain, though not as a player. A Test record which once stood at: Played 13, won 7, lost 2, drawn 4, finished with: Played 39, won 9, lost 10, drawn 20.

Certainly, Gary was a more astute skipper in 1970 than he was in 1965. What, then, was the reason for this deterioration? The answer was that the outstanding players of the great years were beginning to lose a little of their edge and the newcomers were not quite good enough. In this period England beat the West Indies twice, once somewhat fortuitously. Australia trounced them convincingly. India surprisingly won in the West Indies, but then, it should be added, went on to defeat England in England. New Zealand twice held them to a drawn series.

The first serious setback to Gary's career as captain occurred during the 1967–68 MCC tour. The first three Tests were all drawn. In the fourth test Gary declared the West Indies second innings at 92 for 2, setting England to make 215 in two-and-three-quarter hours. England won the match by seven wickets and also captured the Rubber, all as the result of a bold declaration for which Gary was roundly slated.

He was unrepentant, and still is. He cannot see the reason for any controversy, declaring, 'I made that declaration for cricket. If I had not done so the game would have died. This way the West Indies could have won. England had never scored at forty runs an hour during the tour and I did not expect them to do so then.

'Looking back now, what I most remember is that we bowled at about twenty-one overs per hour throughout the innings and, if we had bowled at eighteen, which would have been above average for Test cricket and much quicker than England's rate – even when they employed their spinners – we could easily have drawn the game. That never entered my mind. I was trying to win.'

A cynic might say Gary was naïve, or that he miscalculated, but he definitely gave a practical proof of his principles. Sporting declarations in Test cricket like Gary's in Trinidad, which give the opposition a chance, are very rare. The normal Test match declaration occurs when one team either has established a commanding position or is merely a token gesture after a draw has become inevitable.

There are two main reasons. First, there is the fear of losing and the inevitable inquest which will be held afterwards. Second, a Test match is not complete by itself. It is only one battle in a war which comprises the whole series. Therefore the chief objective is to win the series rather than a particular game. The outcome, of course, has resulted in a high percentage of dull draws, because most international captains prefer to settle for these than to take the chance of making the type of declaration which could possibly end in defeat, not only in the match but also in the Rubber. It may be a narrow view, but it is understandable. In fact, one cannot envisage in any circumstances an England captain, with the Ashes won (providing he does not lose the final Test), taking a similar gamble. It would be entirely different if the only way he could gain the Ashes would be by winning a specific game. Then he might be prepared to throw the match open and risk defeat in seeking victory.

The ideal game is the one that is settled without resource to declarations. There is also nothing wrong with a draw, which can be extremely exciting. However, there are too many drawn Tests which suffer from a surfeit of runs and are dull because the result is predictable from an early stage. Declarations of the type made by Gary at Port of Spain must improve the game as a spectacle and give those watching value for their money. But not many captains are as brave, or, alternatively, as foolish.

MCC's reaction to Gary's challenge was intriguing. They were immediately suspicious, which was hardly surprising because, although they regularly encountered sporting declarations in county cricket, it was entirely foreign to them in Tests. It had to be part of some fiendish plot. They were also worried by the sensational collapse in their first innings which had occurred, somewhat improbably, as a result of the leg-breaks of Basil Butcher. Their immediate reaction was that they might again be bowled out cheaply by the West Indian spinners. However, Geoff Boycott and John Edrich gave them a good start and, as the over rate was sharp and the field an attacking one, runs came briskly. On the departure of the Surrey left-hander, England captain Colin Cowdrey joined the Yorkshire opener. Both were then among the finest players of slow bowling in the world. It was not until the tea interval, however, that it really dawned on the English camp that not only would they avoid defeat but they could win the match in which, up till the closing stages, they had been outplayed. It should be remembered here that, in addition to the controversial declaration with only two wickets down and under a hundred on the board, Gary had also closed his first innings at 526 for 7, which is the type of score normally reckoned to guarantee against defeat.

It can be argued that Gary misread the situation. The pitch played better than he anticipated, while Boycott and Cowdrey batted with more skill and purpose than he had expected. Also, once it became apparent that the West Indies could not bowl out the MCC and the Tourists were going to win, Gary did not have the pace bowlers capable of applying a brake against the flow of runs.

The West Indian press was particularly critical. They had hailed Gary's introduction of Basil Butcher as a bowler as inspired, but they now roundly condemned his declaration as having cost the match and the Rubber. They forgot that he might also have won, and entirely missed what his gesture meant to cricket. Maybe he had been charging at windmills, but it was a gallant charge.

Gary returned for his last time to Australia as captain of the 1968–69 touring party. It was a disappointing trip, with an up-and-coming Australian team comfortably beating an elderly West Indian side on the decline. What the West Indian selectors, including Gary, did not fully appreciate was the extent of the deterioration. The established players failed to return the figures they had in their prime, while the newcomers, in general, did not come up to expectations. It was the end of a great era for West Indian cricket, and Gary was held partially responsible. The truth was that Australia had replaced them as unofficial champions of the world on ability.

Gary believes it might have been a different story if the selectors had not changed the team for the second Test, having won the first, by bringing in inexperienced Charlie Davis for David Holford. Gary has always been one of those people who dislike changing a winning combination. He even went so far as to try to have the decision changed on the morning of the match, urging the need to include a wrist-spinner – by this time a floating bone in the left shoulder prevented him from using himself as a back-of-the-hand bowler – but he was outvoted and his men were routed by the young Australians.

However, the biggest single factor which caused his team to lose the Rubber was, Gary thinks, poor catching. In the five Tests he maintains that the West Indians dropped 34 catches to the Australians' nine!

Critics claimed that on this tour Gary was too remote and spent too much time away from the side. This was due to some extent by the fact that his keenness and considerable skill at golf was not shared by most of his compatriots. It was both noticeable and entirely predictable that the criticism really began to bite when the Tourists started losing. Although there was less team spirit in that West Indian side than existed in some others, the main cause was the lack of form shown by so many of the players. Touring loses much of its attraction for a cricketer when he and his side are not doing as well as he believes they should.

After Australia the West Indies found New Zealand an anti-climax, an entirely predictable reaction which has been shared by every MCC party since 1900. They could, however, only halve the series, and the following summer a weary Sobers was given a new-look side, but one which had a serious basic weakness – insufficient ability – for a short, losing tour of England. He was disappointed at the omission of Edwards, whom he had insisted would do very well in English conditions.

At Lord's, already a Test down, Gary made a beautifully-judged declaration. England could have scored the runs required had they shown more enterprise early on. As it was, they began to accelerate towards a tempting target a shade too late, and just snatched a draw.

He later led the West Indies against India, who somewhat

surprisingly won by one Test, and New Zealand, who
even more surprisingly held them to five high-scoring draws.
Both series were in the Caribbean. By this time too much
cricket had blunted Gary's ability both as a player and
captain. It might have been different if he had been given an
outstanding team and could have afforded to take a less
prominent part in the activities, as had been the case with
Sir Frank Worrell at the end of his career. However, far
from that, Gary was required to score even more runs and
capture more wickets than he had in his prime.

As well as leading the West Indies, Barbados, Nottinghamshire and numerous other teams, he also captained, with
outstanding results, the Rest of the World against both
England and Australia. His task in England was much
easier, and therefore less fun, because he was provided with
such a magnificent team; but his party in Australia contained a number of far less talented performers. The fact
that Gary's multi-racial side was able to defeat Australia –
who do not like losing – provided a splendid example of his
ability as a leader. He moulded his men into a genuine
team, and they gave him tremendous support, none more
so than the white South Africans.

He found skippering the Rest of the World greater fun
than captaining the West Indies because, although the
series were hard-fought, they were taken a shade less
seriously than Tests between countries. There was not quite
the same pressure.

What were Gary's weaknesses as a captain? He was a
logical, practical leader, who put little reliance on instinctive
hunches and was, tactically, closer to Len Hutton than
Richie Benaud. Thus he seldom did the tactically unusual,
and to that extent was predictable. He was perhaps reluctant
to use the non-bowler, as his senses told him that his front-
line bowlers were more likely to succeed. Then he was such
a good player himself that he was inclined to think in terms

24 A bearded Gary, all concentration, in his orthodox slow-left-arm style.

25 The wrist-spinner – bowling for Barbados in 1966.

The triple-purpose bowler

26 In his faster vein : the perfect beginning . . .

27 a flowing follow-through . . .

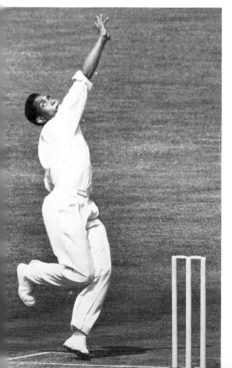

28 . . . and the result : Geoff Boycott trapped in front for a duck during England's first innings in the Third Test at Trent Bridge in 1966. The ball that swung in late was often to find Boycott's weak spot.

of 'the best'. Not unnaturally, he found it difficult to set fields for inaccurate bowling, and he detested bad cricket. He still cannot understand how Boycott lost his wicket, caught on the boundary, attempting to hook the last ball of the day in the 1974 Lord's Test. Earlier in the over Boyce had dropped a bouncer which Boycott had hooked for four, but in the air and close to a square fine-leg. Kanhai's immediate reaction was to post another fielder out on the square leg boundary. Boycott, having ignored a no-balled bouncer, promptly hit the final delivery, another bumper, down the throat of the new fielder. The trap that Kanhai set was not only obvious, but, coming in the last over of the day, should surely have discouraged still further a batsman from taking another chance, hooking. What Gary also found incomprehensible was that Boyce should have bowled, as his last ball of the day, a bouncer – something which had been so blatantly telegraphed. The situation cried out for a yorker.

Gary was not a disciplinarian. He expected complete dedication on the field, and generally gained it. He felt that professional cricketers should have sufficient intelligence to be able to give of their best when playing, but discovered that this was not always the case. He led by personal example rather than command. Although this was completely satisfactory with a talented team, it did not always work where the side was short of class and consequently was inclined to seek excuses for their own deficiencies. Finally, small details have never been his strong point, and it followed that on tour he really needed a manager to tie up the loose ends and occasionally – to switch metaphors – to crack the whip.

Although Gary took his captaincy and responsibilities seriously, he did not allow them to dominate his life off the field. Some skippers are inclined to look upon a tour with the intense passion usually reserved for a religious crusade, and as a result they become so involved that their job is a mental strain. This never happened or could have happened to Gary, because Tests to him were only very important cricket matches to which you gave your all during their progress. They did not warrant undue worry, or sleepless nights.

Yet there were so many advantages in being under his leadership. He was the most complete player ever, who automatically increased the chances of winning by his mere presence. There was also never any question of asking a member of his side to do something he could not do himself, because he was almost invariably their superior with the bat, the ball and in the field. He had, too, a good cricketing brain, able to pick out opposition weaknesses. His field placements were very sound, and his inclination was toward attack whenever feasible, thus pleasing the paying public. His presence at the crease inspired lesser performers – an unusual, almost unique, attribute of a captain. Last of all, as he was completely unselfish and exceptionally loyal to every member of his team, he was liked as a person as well as a skipper, and was, of course, revered as a player. He never spared himself and, perhaps, sometimes attempted to do too much.

At his best his talents were still prodigious, as can be seen from Gary's third tour to England in 1966, when he captained the side, won the series, and scored over 700 runs in the five Tests with an average of more than 100. He also took 20 Test wickets and held some brilliant catches. This consistency, even for him, was astonishing. In the five Tests he notched up three centuries, a ninety and an eighty; he never once failed.

Gary has always maintained that cricket, including Test matches, should be an entertainment, and that the players, if at all possible, should go out of their way to entertain, even if this increased the chances of losing. After all, without public support, the game would die. Nobody can deny that, as player and captain, Gary did his utmost to advance that view.

12

Soldier of Fortune

By the mid-Fifties Gary had established himself as an all-rounder of international calibre who could automatically claim a place on merit in any Test team in the world. When in 1974 a recurrence of his knee injury and the approach of cricketing middle age made him decide to retire from Test cricket he was, even on one leg, a better and more exhilarating player than most people on two. Although he could have gone on longer if he had not experienced that knee trouble, he wisely departed from the international scene as a giant, not as a struggler.

It would have been a fitting climax if his service with the West Indies, which stretched over two decades, had ended at Lord's in 1975 when they so deservedly won the first-ever World Cup, but a minor injury forced him to cry off just before the start of the competition. More than twenty years after his début he was still an automatic choice for the strongest combination in the world! It is hard to say when Gary was at the peak of his powers, but I am inclined to plump for the early and mid-Sixties, especially those two astonishing seasons he spent with South Australia and the Prospect CC.

After that wonderful series between Australia and the West Indies which had resulted in such a dramatic re-awakening of interest in the game, Gary was persuaded to return and play for South Australia, not, at the time, one of the more powerful State sides.

One of the principals behind this move was Sir Donald Bradman, who believed Gary's presence would help to maintain that rekindled interest. He was certainly right, but nobody really expected that the West Indian would do quite so well with both bat and ball. In many ways the Don was the last of Gary's father-figures. Gary admires him enormously – as a person, as the greatest batsman of all time, and for his exceptional knowledge of the game. The Don for his part gave Gary advice and encouragement. He has also said that one of the proudest moments of his entire cricketing life came during the Rest of the World XI's tour of Australia when at their final dinner he was the only guest.

To appreciate Gary's all-round feats Down Under it is necessary to understand that Sheffield Shield cricket is fiercely competitive and also the standard very high. The majority of the pitches are good, so that there are very few easy wickets to be picked up. Conversely, runs have to be earned the hard way, for Australian captains are notoriously parsimonious.

Nevertheless, Gary in 1962–63 became the first cricketer ever to achieve the 'double' of a thousand runs and fifty wickets in a season of first-class cricket – and this despite the fact that Australia has produced some of the finest all-rounders in the game. Nothing illustrates the completeness of his cricket skill more than that feat.

Doing the 'double' in English county cricket – 1000 runs and 100 wickets – was not all that rare. In Australia, however, there are far fewer matches and, generally, much stronger competition. Gary loved his cricket there, not only because the pitches had pace and bounce and the sun usually shone, but because the Aussie approach tended to be more positive and less devious than that of most Englishmen. As a rule their emphasis was more on scoring runs and taking wickets and less on careful accumulation and denial. There were obvious exceptions, but the overall outlook was more West Indian than English and made him feel immediately at home.

I asked Gary what were the main differences between

playing for South Australia and playing for Notts, and why Australia was usually more enjoyable. He gave a number of reasons, which I put down in no particular order of merit. First, he felt the cricket was of a higher standard in all three departments. Second, it was much keener, because there was less of it and the players were consequently never bored. He cannot imagine an Australian State cricketer reacting to a challenging declaration in the same fashion as the Notts professional long before Sobers's time who pleaded to the heavens 'Come on, send it down, I hope it — pours!' The more colourful adjective has been omitted. Third, there was more time available and therefore less sitting back and waiting for declarations. Fourth, the South Australian side was younger and contained fewer married men which, combined with the fact that there were fewer matches, meant the get-togethers after close of play were longer and more enjoyable. Fifth, English county cricket does at times become a bore and a rather pointless exercise. This is seldom allowed to happen in inter-State matches, because they last for four days and are seldom affected by the weather. The players themselves come fresh to each game and are therefore more enthusiastic than their English county counterparts. There are no bonus points for batting. The aim initially is to go for a win on the first innings – which carries points – and then to go for the 'outright'.

Those Aussies who had questioned the wisdom of taking on a West Indian professional were soon forced to have second thoughts, as Gary proceeded not only to score runs and capture wickets with regularity, but to do both in the grand manner. In addition, South Australia, who were one of the weaker states, came close to winning the Sheffield Shield in Gary's first summer, and carried it off in his second.

Their skipper, Les Favell, used to announce to umpires and opponents when making a bowling change: 'From this end "Sobey" bowling chinamen,' or 'Now "Sobey" with the new ball,' or, ' "Sobey" bowling slow left-arm.' He certainly worked 'Sobey', who responded with a dazzling stream of wickets and runs.

The following summer Gary was in even better form with bat and ball. He even managed to improve upon his previous 'double', hitting six centuries, scoring more runs and capturing more wickets than anybody else in Sheffield Shield matches, and seeing his club carry off the trophy.

While in Australia he, like all first-class players, took part in Grade cricket at weekends. This means that he is one of the comparatively few who have participated in senior club cricket in the Caribbean, in Australia and in England. It enables him to make an interesting analysis. The general standard in Australia and Barbados was higher than that in the Lancashire League, for the sound reason that more current, past and coming top-class players were involved. He thought Australian grade cricket had the edge over the West Indian club game, and was played a shade harder. The Australian hated losing, while the West Indian only resented it and tended to forget about it more quickly. The Australian approach was also more professional and meticulous, with compulsory practice, nets and everything starting on time.

The big attraction about our League cricket to Gary and the advantage it had over club games in Barbados and South Australia was the great variety of pitches liable to be encountered – the slow green'un, the pudding, the flier, the road, the beach (which he first encountered at the Oval), the slow lifter, the green top, the crumbler, the dead pitch (where the ball keeps low), and so on. In England a batsman has to know how to make runs on many different kinds of wicket, and a bowler to learn how best to exploit them. As a result of the many years he spent in any country, Gary became a much more complete craftsman than he would have been had his games been mainly played abroad.

When Gary, current captain of the West Indies, signed on for Nottinghamshire in 1968 he became the highest-paid cricketer in the world with a contract the equivalent of £5000 a year, plus rewards from Test cricket and a host of other allied activities. There was considerable competition for his services, since more and more counties were turning to stars from abroad to strengthen their teams and to make them more attractive, and Gary was clearly the finest player they could hope to catch.

Whether the introduction of overseas cricketers has been a good thing for English cricket must be open to considerable doubt. I have never been against the idea in principle, and in fact brought Keith Boyce back from Barbados after I had seen him play out there and before he was a regular member of the Island side, let alone a West Indies player. This is a move neither Essex nor I have ever regretted, as quite apart from his abilities as an all-rounder he has always been such a fine entertainer. However, I do believe that each county should have a limit of one, or at most two players from overseas in their side. This was the original intention, but was abused by the clubs, and the result is the present paucity of good young players produced at home. A couple of years ago I saw a fine match between Kent and Surrey, but no fewer than eight out of the twenty-two taking part had learned their cricket abroad. This is obviously wrong.

In 1968, however, such considerations seemed far away, and Gary went to Notts hoping and expecting to do for them what he had achieved for South Australia a few years earlier. For many reasons this did not work out. It was not that he was a failure with Notts, but, despite being under his leadership and with all his talent, his adopted county were unable to win any of the major honours. This still annoys Gary, because, although they were never an outstanding

side, he feels he should have been able to lift Notts to some
title. He has always been dissatisfied with less than the
best, and this lack of tangible success rankles. Midlands'
cricket and football supporters are inclined to follow a
winning team and, because Notts were not one during
Gary's reign, the crowds never turned up in the numbers
that the presence of the world's finest player warranted.

It all began so auspiciously. Sobers arrived at Trent
Bridge full of confidence, runs, wickets, ideas and enthusiasm.
He was determined to revitalise a county which had finished
fifteenth in the Championship the previous season and were
regularly to be found propping up the foot of the table.

In his first summer he spared himself nothing, amassing
more than 1500 runs to top the Notts batting averages and
picking up 83 wickets. Notts finished a very respectable
fourth, but, despite scoring runs faster and bowling overs
quicker than most sides, their attack was not sufficiently
penetrating to climb higher by winning more matches. Gary
was always willing to set a target, or to chase one, but soon
discovered that many county captains were more cautious
in outlook. However, at the end of that summer the Notts
Committee must have been well pleased with their new
recruit and skipper. He had taken them eleven places up
the table by entertaining cricket, had become the first
person to smash six sixes off one over, and had also struck
the fastest century of the season against Kent, who that year
finished the Championship runners-up.

Everything seemed set for further improvement. Gary
had shown his men that with him around they were capable
of beating anybody. They could be among the winners and
not the also-rans. However, there was one serious snag.
The West Indies, under Gary, were due on a short tour in
1969, which meant that Notts were automatically deprived
of their best batsman, bowler and main inspiration. The
outcome was predictable: the side slipped back. They

dropped to seventh in the table, but did reach the semi-final of the Gillette Cup. But there was always next season, with Gary eager to celebrate his third year with them by capturing one of the honours.

What nobody envisaged was that as a result of government and political pressure not only would the South African Tour to England be called off but that its place would be taken by a Rest of the World XI which Gary was, logically enough, selected to captain. Although he appreciated the honour, and relished the prospect of another series against England, he was also deeply conscious of his debt to Nottinghamshire. He was receiving a very generous salary, and in 1970 he had hoped to cement the start he had made two years earlier by bringing a trophy back to Trent Bridge. He did try to stand down from the World XI, only to be told by the English cricket authorities that if he declined he would not be allowed to turn out for Notts when the Tests were being played. It is easy to understand why Gary was amazed when Geoff Boycott, who had refused to be considered for England, was permitted to play for Yorkshire while the Test matches against Australia were taking place. On the other hand, without him the World XI would have lost credence as a serious replacement for the South African Test series. It could not have been properly termed 'the Rest of the World' if it did not include the first choice for such a team. Also, had Gary been allowed to withdraw, other counties might well have refused their overseas players, which would have killed the whole operation.

With their captain and star performer missing for about half the Championship games because he was leading the Rest of the World, the Notts revival did not occur. They won only four games, gates dwindled, membership dropped and interest waned.

Wisden has this to say about Gary and the county: 'It was a matter for comment that he nearly always reserved his best performances for his appearances against England. Throughout the season he only managed to capture 43 wickets and these cost him 25 runs each, which for a player of Sobers's ability was poor.' The criticism, both implied and stated, was less than fair. Everybody, especially the Editor of *Wisden*, should know that great players tend to rise to big occasions. Therefore it was in no way surprising that Gary should shine more brightly in the challenging atmosphere of a Test than in a county game at Trent Bridge before a few men and a dog.

The cost of his wickets that summer does seem expensive, until one takes into consideration the ultra-perfect pitches at Nottingham, the fact Gary was now only fast-medium and the insipid quality of the rest of the attack. The placidness of the pitch is further reflected by the high scores and averages returned by some quite ordinary batsmen in the county XI and the fact that all his main bowling colleagues returned far worse figures. He himself comfortably topped the club's batting with an average in the upper seventies.

In 1971 after two interrupted summers Gary was at last available to devote his full attention to Nottinghamshire cricket, but the expected improvement in the club's fortunes did not occur and they experienced a horrid spell in which they could only win one of their first sixteen Championship games, were knocked out in the first round of the Gillette Cup and lost eight consecutive Sunday League matches. This was followed by a remarkable revival which emphasised the narrowness of the margin that divides success from failure. If only they had shown that type of form at the commencement of the season it could easily have been an entirely different story.

Not surprisingly, Gary himself was stale from too much cricket and failed to receive the support from some members of his team and of the committee when he needed it most. There was considerable sniping behind his back and one was left wondering whether he was perhaps not too nice and too honest a person to captain a team when luck was not on his side. He has always loved cricket, but has never relished the dirty in-fighting which so often occurs in sport in these circumstances.

It was easy to understand why in the following year he gave up the captaincy to Brian Bolus, who had been his deputy, but whose approach to the game was far more dour, as one might have expected from his Yorkshire background. Gary was having problems with his knee, was obviously tired both physically and mentally, was becoming slightly disillusioned, and some of the initial enthusiasm must have departed.

The knee, which had been causing trouble for some time, eventually became so painful that he had an operation, which caused him to miss almost the whole of the 1972 season. Gary does not subscribe to the accepted view that this injury was the direct outcome of too much cricket and too much wear and tear. He believes it was the result of Sunday Cricket, which artificially restricts a bowler's run-up to ten paces. Although he had, for a quick bowler, a very short approach, this still had to be reduced for John Player League matches. The result was that he lost some of the rhythm from which his pace was derived. In an effort to maintain the same pace he was forced to rely to a greater extent on brute force, and his knee simply gave way under the additional strain.

In 1973 Gary led Notts for the last time and was given what must surely have been one of the weakest teams to have ever represented the county. It came as no surprise to anybody that they should have finished at the bottom of the table, although if Gary had not been called up for three Tests by the West Indies they would probably have escaped that indignity. He himself was so out of touch in the early part of the season that his selection surprised him. However, the West Indies selectors were only too aware of how he reacted to the challenge of the big time. Their judgment proved right, and he once again played an important part in the rout of England.

Jack Bond was appointed captain, manager, coach and general factotum in 1974, a move which baffled everybody, apart from those who made it. Bond was a competent county batsman who had enjoyed great success as captain of Lancashire in limited-over cricket, for which they were so well equipped. As captain of Notts he was bound to fail, because Notts were at best an indifferent side and certainly could not afford the luxury of carrying somebody who was not really worth his place even with them. Gary played out his last summer for Notts against this slightly pathetic background. Once again he headed their batting with an average of 48, and hit the fastest century of the season, which was made – typically – against Derbyshire, who had one of the most powerful attacks of all the counties. However, his bowling had by now lost some of its penetration, and although still very useful was no longer devastating. He felt the time had come to retire from county cricket, which contained so many games and variety of game that he was beginning to lose some of his zest. He had always believed that there was no point in playing if it was not enjoyable and there were times with Notts when the pleasure was at best minimal, especially on those occasions when there was nothing at stake.

Had Gary been able to devote an entire season to Notts in his second or third year with them they might have gone close to winning something, but by the time he departed not only were his own all-round talents less, but there simply was not sufficient support available to make any serious impression either in the Championship or the Sunday League. The only serious hopes were in the knock-out tournaments, where odd things do occur.

Although he enjoyed the 40-over games and appreciated their financial importance, he much preferred first-class cricket, or one-day matches of longer duration, where the all-out slog for runs had a less important role. Notts could have done well in either the Gillette Cup or the Benson and Hedges Trophy had they enjoyed the kind of luck which took Middlesex to two finals in 1975, and had Gary himself struck top form at the right moment. But it never happened.

Gary liked living in Nottinghamshire, and Pru, by that time his wife, was particularly impressed by the area and its people. But then Nottingham is one of the most attractive cities in England; and Gary would be happy in most places.

13

Love and Marriage

Top-class professional cricket is a great life for the single man. Although he cannot hope to make a fortune, like a boxer, golfer, jockey, tennis player or soccer star, he earns enough to live comfortably. He also has the considerable satisfaction of being paid for doing something he loves and which, if he were less proficient, he would pay to do. There is the opportunity of numerous trips overseas under ideal conditions, and at someone else's expense. Providing he is an easy mixer, he need never be lonely, because the companionship of his colleagues is readily available.

If he wants female company there is never any shortage. A certain amount of glamour still surrounds an international sportsman, so that should he lack the inclination or confidence to go looking for 'talent' he can always turn to one of the camp-followers who are inevitably to be found. They do not appear in the droves which follow pop entertainers, but they are about.

Unlike the footballer the cricketer is not hemmed in by tight training regulations. He can afford a perfectly normal existence and still turn in good performances on the field. It is often said that a newly married footballer always loses his edge, and that it takes about a season before he recovers his pre-married form, while boxers usually settle for a monastic life before a big fight. In sharp contrast, there is a widely-held view among cricketers, particularly supported by batsmen, that sexual intercourse is a help before a long innings. The actual phrase is 'clears the eye'.

As far as alcohol is concerned, the footballer will have the occasional drink, but over the years fast bowlers have been encouraged to drink beer – and have certainly put away some pints.

The answer, of course, is that it is not feasible to train to a peak for a game which can last for five days and which is often played seven days a week. There is the occasional fitness fanatic, but the chances are he will not be temperamentally suited to the sport.

The snag occurs when a cricketer marries and has to take on such responsibilities as a wife, a mortgage and children. Even the most tolerant wife is seldom pleased at the prospect of losing her spouse for five months while he enjoys himself in Australia or other far-away, sunny lands. She will also never completely understand how apparently adult and intelligent males can go on talking about a game of cricket until the sun comes up. It may, too, take her a little time to digest that, though the match ended at 6 p.m., the ensuing celebrations required a slight delay of some six hours! She will learn to read instinctively whether her mate has scored a hundred, or whether he has failed to register and is therefore unlikely to be the most lively of companions for some time.

A professional cricketer's wife has her problems, and whoever remarked that no full-time cricketer should ever marry undoubtedly had a point. It is noticeable that those with daughters tend to say, 'I hope she doesn't marry a cricketer.' The mothers are more vehement.

Gary did not rush into marriage. He liked his way of life and his freedom, and there was never any shortage of girl friends. He also appreciated that matrimony would provide more problems for him than it would for the normal professional player. He had no permanent base and, although his real home was in Barbados, he spent more time in England. A permanent union, if not to be avoided, was to be entered upon slowly and with care.

He became seriously emotionally involved twice, once in

Australia and once in Barbados. Marriage was contemplated, but never materialised. Then, while touring India, he became engaged to a beautiful Indian film star, Anju Mahendru, who was just beginning to make a name for herself in pictures. It was great publicity and a natural story – 'Handsome West Indian cricket captain to wed up-and-coming actress.' She was to join him when he returned to England after the tour, but the romance proved short-lived. There were problems, including films to be made, and her family, who encouraged the friendship, were less enthusiastic about a wedding.

Gary's career as a gay and carefree bachelor was finally brought to an end by Miss Pru Kirby, whom he married in England on 11 September, 1969. I have put in the date as a reminder to Gary, because he is inclined to be forgetful over such matters as anniversaries.

It was a happy and wise decision. By that time Gary was beginning to drift, unsure where he was heading, or if he wanted to go there anyway. His marriage to Pru gave him a new sense of purpose, a stability, and later a family.

Why he fell in love with an attractive blonde Australian is easy to understand. The 'how' provides surprises. Most people assumed when they heard Gary was to wed an Australian girl that the two had met on one of his tours Down-Under, and that she was a keen cricket follower. They could not have been further from the truth.

Pru, a well-educated, independent girl with a typical middle-class background, had followed the almost standard practice for an Australian female in her late teens or early twenties – to go on a European 'walk-about'. Like many others, she decided she wanted to see something of the world before she settled down, and therefore went on a prolonged working holiday which took in both Canada and Great Britain.

While in England she found a job with the Australian

Gary in charge

29 As captain of the West Indies, he introduces C.A. Davis to the Queen during the second Test Match against England in 1969.

30 (*above*) Gary takes the field as Captain of Notts during a 1968 match against Lancashire. Behind him is Maurice Hill. **31** (*left*) A cheerful Sobers leads his powerful Barbados team off to another match. Under his captaincy they won the Shell Shield, and he also had the unique distinction of leading Barbados against the Rest of the World.

32 (*above*) The two greatest : The 'Muhammad Ali' of cricket chats with his boxing *alter ego* at Lord's in 1966. Looking on is Gary's brother Gerry.

33 (*left*) With Indian film star Anju Mahindu who, at 17, became engaged to Gary during his visit to India in 1967.

34 In 1969 Gary became involved in 'Two Gentlemen Sharing', a film starring Robin Philips, Judy Geeson and Hal Frederick, in which he 'ghosted' a cricket scene.

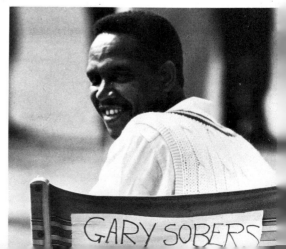

GARY SOBERS

Canned Fruit Industry which enabled her to explore the country still further. At that time they were carrying out a special public relations exercise which attracted local publicity and was intended to link English people with friends and relatives in Australia. Messages were taped in a special caravan that was moved to a new city each week, and were then relayed across the world. The whole operation was naturally tied up with a big sales drive in each of the areas visited.

Pru's particular job was to go ahead of the main party in a jeep, to contact VIPs, tie up details and arrange the local publicity. One of the names on her Nottingham list was Gary Sobers, a name which at the time meant absolutely nothing to her. It is a fallacy to imagine that every Australian loves cricket and knows something about the game.

A letter had been previously sent to Gary. This, predictably, had not been answered, so Pru made her way to Trent Bridge and spoke to the Secretary. She asked him whether Gary would tape a message to friends in Australia. He said he could see no problems, and, pointing out the club captain, suggested that she asked him in person. It was their first meeting.

Gary agreed immediately. As he says, 'Pretty blondes don't come up and ask you to send messages to Australia every day. You got to make the most of it when they do.'

After everything had been fixed, Gary asked Pru whether she would like to have a drink with him that evening – he was always a firm believer in not missing chances – and Pru accepted. She liked his style, his voice and looks, but, equally important, it was her first night in a strange city and she had no other engagement. The big romance, although neither of them thought of it in that light for some considerable time, had begun.

Pru's job took her from town to town and fate conspired that a high percentage of these trips coincided with Gary's

s.g.–ɪ

itinerary, or were within easy reach of Nottinghamshire. As a result Pru and Gary saw a great deal of each other – in fact, there was only one weekend on which they were unable to meet.

Although they enjoyed each other's company and had a good time together, Pru never seriously considered marriage, even though Gary, with commendable foresight, did bring up the matter on several occasions. Pru liked Gary enormously, but did not view him as her future husband. He was generous, a fine host, attentive, different from her other admirers, a very good dancer, possessed an infectious laugh and plainly loved life. She was never in any way concerned by the difference in the colour of their skins. But she saw their relationship as a pleasant interlude between two people from different countries who were having fun in another land; nothing more.

Pru had decided long before they met that she would return to Australia at the end of the summer, and the fact that Gary happened to be going to captain the West Indies out there was coincidental. He was naturally delighted at the chance to see her again so soon, and wanted her to fly home, but Pru decided to travel back by ship which would give her time to think things out.

Pru came from a good and happy Australian home. Her father was intelligent and had fought his way up. He possessed a keen mind and, although largely self-taught, became something of a literary and mathematical scholar. In his daughter's words 'He was a little pedantic, perhaps, but very loving, understanding and fair. My mother worshipped him.'

In her letters to her parents from England Pru had casually mentioned Gary several times and had suggested to him he should look them up when he arrived in Australia with his team. She had also told her mother of his fondness for rice, ice-cream, whisky and tabasco sauce. When he phoned her parents from Sydney soon after landing there was considerable excitement in the Kirby household, as captains of touring teams do not come to dinner every day. Mrs Kirby dashed out and bought some tabasco sauce and Mr Kirby unveiled his special bottle of Johnny Walker Black. At this stage Pru was still abroad.

The first meeting between her parents and Gary proved a happy occasion, and was followed by a highly successful meal, even if Gary did find tabasco sauce and ice-cream a slightly unusual pairing. The Kirbys took to him instinctively, and he to them, while the Johnny Walker Black helped to cast a mellow glow over the proceedings. Gary told them outright he wanted to marry their daughter, and as he drove Gary back to the airport that evening Pru's father summed up the situation as he saw it as an Australian: 'Son, if Pruey wants to marry you I'll do everything in my power to dissuade her. But, damn it, I like you, you bastard!'

It should be appreciated that in Melbourne the colour question hardly exists. This is mainly due to the white immigration policy and to the fact that the coloured minority remains so small. Problems of colour and race usually occur only when the minority group has settled in sufficient numbers as to be noticed against the main bulk of the population: twenty or thirty years ago, for instance, the racial tension which can be found in some towns in England today was completely unknown. The Kirbys, like most Australians, fancied themselves unbiased lovers of all mankind, irrespective of colour or creed, but this did not stretch to the extent of wanting their daughter to take part in a mixed marriage. It had nothing to do with Gary as a person, but the idea was entirely foreign to their way of life. They also feared that any future grandchildren could be handicapped because of the colour of their skin.

When the ship that had brought Pru from England reached Australia she was met by her father and also, much

to her surprise, by Gary, who had flown especially from
Brisbane. She was delighted to find how well the two men
in her life got on, but her reunion with Gary did not go
smoothly. It all seemed different back in her own environment, and this effectively soured the happy relationship they
had enjoyed together in England. The outcome was a
blazing row.

Gary returned to his team disappointed and upset because
he had been hoping Pru would agree to become engaged.
The affair appeared irrevocably over, which in some respects pleased her parents, but worried Pru. Although she
did not want to marry Gary, she liked him a great deal and
felt she owed him something for the good times they had had
abroad. Above all she did not want to hurt him, so she wrote
to say that she was prepared to go out with him when he
came back to Melbourne, but on the clear understanding
there would be no more talk of marriage.

Gary jumped at the opportunity to forget the quarrel and
start again. The romance between them grew, and Pru's
intentions were soon forgotten. As she put it, 'We were
dancing on New Year's Eve and, as I looked up at him, I
suddenly thought to myself, "I do love that guy".' From
that moment it was just a matter of time before they were
married, because Pru was, and is, a very determined young
lady, and such women seldom fail to achieve what they have
set their hearts on. When she told Gary that she was willing
to get married he was delighted, but, being typically male,
was not quite so enthusiastic about setting an actual date. It
is one thing to propose; it is another matter when the girl
accepts, possibility turns into reality and there is no turning
back.

They became officially engaged and agreed that they
would marry in England after the cricket season. Gary
returned to England first, to lead the West Indies on their
short tour, and was later joined by Pru.

An international cricket captain with a fiancée in tow is hardly the ideal combination. Gary already had more than enough to do keeping his players contented, but there were no major problems – Gary would probably not have noticed them anyway, and Pru has tact. In the second half of the summer he resumed with Notts, and soon after the season ended Pru Kirby became Pru Sobers. They married for the best of reasons: they were in love, and it was a move which definitely suited Gary.

The quality which appealed most to Pru at the start, and which still does, is Gary's basic simplicity – he is straightforward and honest, with no complicated hang-ups or prejudices. Talking to me many years later and discussing their first meeting Pru said: 'When I first met Gary back in 1968 I was silently amazed at how unspoilt and sincere a man he was for one who had achieved so much fame. It was as if he had created a basic code for himself and lived by it unflinchingly. It enabled him to be as at home whether having "peas and rice" with the very poor, or caviare with princes.'

In the early days of their marriage, however, Pru discovered his uncomplicated approach to life, although relaxing, could also be frustrating. Through her own up-bringing and subsequent travels she had developed several tastes of her own. These were so different from those of her husband that it was inevitable their outlook and interests would often not coincide. She tried unsuccessfully to introduce to him some of her ideas but it was a long time before she realised and accepted that in certain areas communication between them would always be difficult. In the West Indies Pru has to endure endless discussions about cricket, far more than she would normally encounter in England or Australia. When Gary was actively playing first-class cricket, and before their children were born, Pru would attend most of the games, but it is not her scene, and has been something she has had to learn to accept.

Gary, for his part, is a tolerant husband, especially about material things, is naturally kind and very generous. Whenever away from home he will spend a small fortune on phone calls. Like most West Indian fathers he adores his two sons, Matthew and Daniel, who in turn worship him. On the other hand, his way of life has meant that he has often had to be absent and naturally has not seen as much of his boys as Pru. He has displayed domestic talents, however, which might surprise many who know him, proving both a competent nappy-changer and an uncomplaining night-feeder.

To Pru Gary's biggest weakness is his laziness, which, if one considers his non-stop efforts as a cricketer, is perhaps strange. But Gary's particular brand of sloth is mental, not physical. He has never disciplined himself sufficiently to write things down, with the result that he is forgetful. To make matters worse, Gary hates saying 'No' when somebody asks him to do something. He will undertake a commitment with the best possible intentions, but unless he is continually reminded, preferably by phone and personal contact, it is all too possible that he will forget.

It has been a marriage of opposites and, as is so often the case, has drawn strength from this. Quite apart from the difference in background, upbringing and environment, their basic characters are far apart. Gary has always been an easy-going, easy-mixing, party-loving person, while Pru by nature is introspective, quieter, fairly fastidious, artistic. He loves talking with people anywhere and anytime. She is less outgoing and far more particular. He has come to rely and depend on her judgment to a considerable extent, for she has a sound, hard, practical streak; his decisions are apt to be instinctive, hers are usually weighed and analysed. This was noticeable in their courtship. Gary wanted to get married immediately; it was Pru who took time to consider the pros and the cons. Both have a keenly developed taste for clothes and regard for their appearance. They are always impeccably dressed and their own well-turned-out look is reflected in their children and home. When Gary sees something which appeals, he will buy it without counting the cost. Pru will always ask the price.

Gary and Pru have now been married six years, and during this period they have had to face the problems of bringing up a family without a permanent home, because they have seldom been able to stay in one spot for more than six months at a time. They will probably settle in Barbados, where understandably Gary has become a living legend. Pru has already grown to love the island, which is cosy, civilised, and with an almost perfect climate. She has also been well received by all the community and as an Australian especially appreciates the easy informality that exists. She has already made many close friends, many of whom have no direct connection with the world of cricket. Yet although Pru and Gary have their own special interests they have become a team, drawing strength from one another. It is a good marriage.

14

The Rhodesian Affair

In September 1970 Gary brought his wife home to Barbados to find that the knives were out – long ones. The offence for which he was indicted was playing in a two-day, double-wicket cricket competition in Rhodesia. This was to cause a furore throughout the Caribbean and provided an especially unpleasant example of how easily sport can be exploited by politicians. For nearly two months Gary's brief two-day visit to Rhodesia created so much controversy and bitterness that West Indian cricket was nearly split asunder. It caused the cancellation of the 1971 Indian tour, and was partially responsible for Gary's premature retirement as captain of the West Indies.

We shall never know for certain, but I am cynical enough to believe that if Gary had come back as a triumphant hero instead of a defeated captain the outcry would have been far less. As a result of the West Indies having lost to England there were those in cricket circles who felt that the time had come for the king to abdicate. They joined forces with those who were genuinely incensed by his Rhodesian visit and the much larger group who simply used the affair for their own ends. By fanning the flames of the controversy some cricket administrators and followers – not, I might add, the players – saw an excellent opportunity of ousting Sobers from the captaincy.

The story began when Gary was leading the Rest of the World, and Eddie Barlow, one of his team, suggested he might take part in a double-wicket tournament in Rhodesia.

The idea appealed to Gary, and he decided to accept. He was, it should be remembered, a private individual and a professional who earned his money by playing cricket. He would, perhaps, have been wiser if he had discussed the trip with some of the West Indian officials who were over in England that summer and who, because they were living permanently in the Caribbean, would probably have seen the danger.

The news that Sobers had accepted an invitation to partner Ali Bacher in the double-wicket competition was announced on 7 September by Reuter. On 8 September, in England, the *Daily Express* editorial said that 'the great majority of British sports fans will applaud him for making such a personal decision without prejudice,' which was the view of most Englishmen. In Barbados Peter Short, Secretary of the West Indian Board of Control, issued a statement to the effect that the decision was entirely Gary's own and had nothing to do – as was fairly obvious – with the Board. It was also pointed out that he was playing as a professional and as an individual. This was something often ignored in the ensuing rumpus.

On 9 September a dispatch from London questioned the secrecy which had surrounded the affair. On 11 September Gary flew into Seawell to be met by friends and a large contingent from the media, who never fail to sniff out a controversial story. On this occasion they could hardly have failed to do so. Earlier that day Frank Walcott, leader of the Barbados Labour Party, issued a strongly-worded statement condemning Sobers's action which, he said, disqualified him from leading the West Indies. He went on to wonder what Sobers was attempting to prove and whether he wanted to show that Ian Smith and his white Rhodesians were not so bad after all, or that leading West Indians were totally unaware of serious world affairs. He declared that, because Gary was acclaimed by all West Indians as their symbol of world fame and equality, 'He cannot lapse into any area which is an offence to the dignity and character of West Indians.'

It was all strongly emotive stuff made, significantly, before Gary had even arrived back. It was also carefully calculated to provide Walcott with more news coverage than anything he had ever said before. What is surprising is that this attack should have come from a Bajan, who should surely have known better than most that Gary, throughout his long career, had never done any really mean act, which cannot be said about many people, and even fewer politicians.

At an impromptu conference at the airport Gary told the press why he had gone to Rhodesia. 'I thought at first it would be a very good thing for me, because I am a cricketer and I personally think of cricket, not politics. I thought that to go to Rhodesia would possibly do some good, considering the problems that they had with the South African team not coming to England.'

It would be wrong to imagine that Gary was insensitive to the feelings of other West Indians, but he knew that in the brotherhood of cricket there were no insuperable barriers, social or ethnic. He had just led a team of liquorice-all-sorts in complete harmony. When Pakistan and India were at war Hanif Mohammed and the Nawab of Pataudi played in the same cricket team. For Hampshire, a South African, Richards, and a West Indian, Greenidge, formed the most devastating opening partnership in the world. One of the finest tributes ever paid to South African Graeme Pollock, after he had scored a superb century off a West Indian team at Scarborough, was their judgment in the dressing-room that Sobers could not have played a better innings.

Gary's passionate love for the sport and his desire that white and black should play together as they do in England blinded him to the fact that the brotherhood of man is not so tolerant as the brotherhood of cricket. For that error of judgment some of his own people did their best to crucify him.

In retrospect it is easy to say that Gary was unwise to have gone to Rhodesia, but of course he never intended, nor expected, to upset anybody. He genuinely thought he was aiding the cause of multi-racial sport in Africa. He showed an appealing naïvety, perhaps, but then he is basically a straightforward individual without guile or deviousness. Certainly he emerged from the affair with honour, which is more than can be said for those who became involved in it for publicity's sake.

Gary returned to Barbados on 13 September to a reception which was less friendly than he would normally have expected; the poison had begun to spread. In Antigua, the *Workers' Voice*, firmly controlled by the ruling Labour Party, came out with one of the more fatuous statements – and there were to be many – that Sobers was 'a white black man'. They also stated that he had abdicated his loyalty to Africans everywhere by playing in Rhodesia, which to anybody who knew or knows Gary is absurd.

One of the unintentional pieces of humour occurred on 17 September when Conrad Hunte, trying to be absolutely honest as befits a disciple of Moral Rearmament, said the important thing was not whether Gary was right or wrong, but whether he had changed Ian Smith, or *vice versa*. The likelihood of either happening in their short meeting still makes me chuckle. Some fairly influential and crafty people have tried without conspicuous success to change Ian Smith, while Gary will surely remain essentially the same until he dies.

By now it was open season for Gary-sniping. The Editor of the *Guyana Chronicle*, whom few know and even fewer are likely to remember, pontificated in the grand manner: 'If Sobers does not appreciate what being a leader is, then he should not be entrusted with leadership.' He, like others,

conveniently overlooked the fact that Gary was appointed
to captain a cricket team – which he did rather better than
most – and not to lead an ideological crusade.

Jamaica's Minister of State, Hector Whynter, was another
who saw fit to take Gary to task. One wonders whether he
would have adopted the same attitude if Gary had been a
Jamaican. There is not always complete harmony between
the islands, and the opportunity to have a dig is seldom
neglected. On 10 September, the Prime Minister of Guyana,
Forbes Burnham, demanded an apology from Sobers for 'his
foolish and ill-advised stand' or there would be no welcome
for him in Guyana. The affair then descended to black
farce, with the Guyana Cricket Board of Control – 'control'
not being especially noticeable in this instance – also calling
for an apology.

Barbados by this time was understandably somewhat
sickened by the abuse that was being aimed at one of her
chosen sons. Their Deputy Prime Minister, Cameron Tudor,
said that the criticism was out of all proportion to the offence.
He went on to add, 'To say, as some say who should know
better, that he would not be welcomed in their country is an
affront to the people of Barbados.'

However, by this time it was too late. The censure which
had started as an insignificant snowball had turned into an
avalanche threatening the existence of West Indian cricket.
Jamaica's two major political parties joined together to
attack Sobers as if he were a criminal, instead of an innocent
at large in a highly prejudiced world, who had erred in his
judgment – and then only according to some people, but
certainly not everyone.

Hugh Shearer of the Labour Party demanded that Gary
should resign the captaincy of the West Indies, while
Michael Manley said that, unless Sobers apologised, 'he
may not be welcomed anywhere by people who believe that
justice is bigger than even sport'.

A day later, on 15 October, the newspaper of Dr Cheddi Jagan's Progressive Party came out demanding Gary's resignation and the Guyana Cricket Board held an indecisive meeting on the position.

Next, Peter Short, then Secretary of the Board, confirmed that Forbes Burnham was demanding an apology, which left the WICBC in the invidious and unusual position that their own captain might not be allowed into Guyana. It was becoming nastier all the time, and Gary himself could not see why he should apologise for doing something which he had considered at the time to be right.

On 21 October Lionel Craig tabled a resolution in the House of Assembly deploring the action of the Guyana Prime Minister. Something had to be done to ease the tension building up between the islands, and preferably before some undiplomatic individual came out with what many people were thinking and answered the Burnham statement that Gary was not welcome in Guyana with 'Who wants to go there anyway?' That would have meant the end of inter-island first-class cricket for a few seasons.

On 25 October there was an emergency meeting of the WICBC with Gary, which ended up with a statement by Sobers on that Rhodesian trip, which was not in fact an apology, but sufficiently resembled one to enable Burnham to accept it without loss of face.

This point was made clear by Errol Barrow, Prime Minister of Barbados, who deliberately countered the BBC's broadcast assertion that Sobers had apologised with a statement that the WICBC had never asked for one. This was important because, although Gary wanted peace and harmony, he has always been a man of high principle. He was prepared to compromise, but not to make a full apology for what he saw, at most, as an error of judgment. Here is his letter to the President of the WICBC:

Dear Mr President,

When I accepted the invitation to take part in a two-day double-wicket competition in Rhodesia I was assured that there was no segregation in sport in that country, but I was not made aware of the deep feelings of the West Indian people. I have since learnt of this feeling and the wider international issues involved.

I am naturally deeply distressed by, and concerned over, the tremendous controversy and bitterness which have arisen after my return from Salisbury.

As I was not aware of the serious repercussions, I may have expressed myself in such a way as to create the impression of indifference to these issues.

Mr President, I wish to inform you in all sincerity that this is far from my true feelings, as the prestige of West Indian cricket and the unity and dignity of West Indian and African people are interests I have always served.

I therefore wish to convey to you and the members of the Board my sincere regrets for any embarrassment which my action may have caused and to assure you of my unqualified dedication whenever I may be called upon to represent my country, the West Indies, and my people.

Signed G. A. SOBERS.

It is a masterly letter and, although the thoughts are those of Gary, they had been drafted by a more subtle hand. It achieved its objective and the controversy ended. It was accepted by Forbes Burnham, who assured Gary of a warm welcome when he next came to Guyana.

Gary would not tell me who masterminded the document, but I cannot help feeling it contains more than a touch of the diplomatic wisdom of the Prime Minister of Barbados.

Throughout this unpleasant period it should not be thought that Gary lacked supporters. His friends – in other words everyone who knew him well – realised he had never intended to do any harm or upset anyone. The cricket writer Brunell Jones summed things up aptly when he wrote 'The least Sobers's tormentors could have done was to respect the man's judgment, even if they did not agree with it.'

The Opposition Leader in Trinidad praised the calmness of Sobers 'when faced by the primitive savagery of West Indian gutter politicians'. He might have gone on to add that a person who never flinched from fast bowling was certainly not going to run from a political barrage of beamers and bouncers.

15
End of an Era

One of the most surprising features of Gary's long cricket career is that, although he never spared himself on the field and lived a very full life off it, he missed very few matches. For almost two decades he never missed a Test for the West Indies and after the retirement of Frank Worrell captained the side for 39 games on the trot.

People were forever predicting that he would burn himself out, but this did not happen. Sometimes he suffered from a surfeit of the game and more than once he played when not completely fit. Even when not one hundred per cent he was more effective than most.

What eventually caused him to abdicate from the captaincy – apart from the Rhodesian rumpus – and to retire from the first-class and international scene earlier than he wanted was a recurrence of a knee injury which started back in the early Sixties. The knee was successfully operated on in 1962 and Gary recovered very quickly to play, arguably, the finest cricket of his life with South Australia. Several years later, as I have mentioned, a floating bone in his left shoulder caused him to lose his googly, but with his batting, seam and orthodox spin he still remained the most complete all-rounder in the world.

However, in the early Seventies he began to feel twinges. He believed this was due to the limited run-up in the Sunday games rather than to overwork, and carried on with a dodgy knee for a couple of seasons. I have never found any great difficulty in batting with a physical disability, but it is a very different matter when it comes to bowling with a strained or

35 Gary Sobers and Graham Pollock, West Indian and South African together, leave the field at the end of play during the fifth Test at the Oval between England and the Rest of the World in 1970. The two best left-handers in the world scored 88 in an hour's magic in the day's final session.

36 Later that year, the start of the storm : Gary shakes hands with Mrs Ian Smith while her husband looks happily on.

37 Pru Kirby, public relations girl, meets Gary Sobers, international cricket star.

38 A happy family. Gary and Pru in February 1975 with their sons Matthew and Daniel.

pulled muscle. You cannot put that little extra into your bowling, and this makes all the difference. As it was, the knee got steadily worse, and in the summer of 1972 Gary had to have a second operation, which prevented him playing for Notts and made his chances of representing the West Indies against Australia in the Caribbean the following winter very doubtful.

The West Indies Board chose five players currently with English counties to come back and take part in the series. Gary told the President of the Board that he did not expect them to pay his passage home, as he was unsure of his fitness, but that he was going back to Barbados anyway and, if he felt he had fully recovered, he was willing to be considered for selection.

His successor as captain had to be considered. There were some, indeed, who felt this desirable because West Indian cricket was going through a sticky patch and even a completely fit Sobers was not quite the force he had once been.

Gary's three choices for the man to take over are interesting. He plumped first for his cousin David Holford, not on the grounds of nepotism but because he considered him to be the soundest skipper in the West Indies. Second in line he placed Clive Lloyd, the present holder, who was not at that time much favoured outside of Guyana. Gary had, however, recognised his potential as a captain and batsman, and also saw the advantage of gambling on a young candidate with a future which looked much brighter than Holford's. His third choice was Rohan Kanhai because of his extensive knowledge of the game, the fact that he was still an outstanding player and had a splendid long-service record.

As it was likely to be only a temporary appointment Rohan was the man the selectors eventually appointed. The next question was: would Gary recover in time to play against Australia in the first Test in Jamaica? He had had the advantage of having faced Lillee, then rated the main menace, but he feared his knee might give way and wisely was not considered.

In preparation for the next Test Gary turned out for Barbados against Trinidad, opened the bowling in the first innings and was quite happy with his performance. He declined to bowl in the second because the troubled knee, not unexpectedly, felt a little sore. He instead took things fairly easily, fielded at slip and thought, by and large, it had been a very satisfactory return and that he would be fit to take his accustomed place in the Barbados Test. He also decided that, having come through one contest without mishap, it would be foolish to risk aggravation by playing in the Barbados game against the Tourists which immediately preceded the Test. The selectors thought otherwise.

Just before the Island's match with the Aussies Jeffrey Stollmeyer came into the dressing-room and asked Gary if he intended to take part. Gary said it would be better if he did not play, so that he could be completely fit for the second Test. He was then presented with an ultimatum – either he played for Barbados or he would not be considered for the Test which followed. This incensed Gary, who had never let his country down in any game and felt he was the best judge of his own fitness. He did not play.

He was left out of the second Test, although good use could have been made of his services. Julien, his logical substitute, injured a finger just before the start and Boyce was brought in at the last minute. The WICBC stated that the medical report about Sobers's knee indicated he might not be completely fit for Test cricket, but obviously seven months after the operation there was only one person really capable of deciding, and that was Gary himself. It was something of a slight to a man who had played over 150 innings for his country and scored more runs than anyone else in West Indian history.

Having sat out the match as a spectator Gary was then

asked to play in a two-day game, which he considered an insult, quite apart from proving nothing. He refused – with the result that he was never considered for the rest of the series, which Australia went on to win 3–0 with two drawn. The completeness of their victory came as a distinct surprise, because it was achieved without the help of Lillee or Massie, while Mallett had been unable to make the trip. The Australians had plenty of batting, but few people – even the Australians themselves – would have fancied Walker, Hammond and Jenner to pick up such a rich harvest of wickets. The truth was that the West Indies, collectively and individually, failed to do themselves justice, although the leadership of Kanhai impressed, and he was appointed skipper for the tour to England that followed.

In view of Sobers's form with bat and ball for the West Indies against England only a few months later, his presence and ability would probably have been enough to have gained his side victory in both the third and the fourth Tests, both lost by narrow margins to the Aussies. Although the knee never completely recovered and slowed him down to some extent, the fact remains that even with a handicap he was still a very fine player and certainly worth a Test place on merit. The Bajan Secretary for Sport, Dennis Hunte, put it more bluntly when he declared Gary's treatment by the WICBC was abhorrent – 'because Sobers on one leg is better than anyone else in the team'.

Gary is convinced that from the second Test on he was fit to play for the West Indies – not as fit as he had been in the past, but still able to stand up to the demands of international cricket. This he was to demonstrate the following summer in England.

The selectors understandably had their doubts. They were afraid that Gary was not fit enough to do either himself or the West Indies full justice on the field. It was an understandable point of view, but in Gary's case proved a psychological error. Had they been dealing with anyone else they would have been right. But I would always take a gamble on Gary, who would never be prepared to appear in front of his own people in a vital Test unless certain he could perform to his own high standards. He believed that, although less mobile in the field and between the wickets and his bowling now no more than fast-medium, he was still capable of playing a decisive part at international level. His presence would have made an enormous difference when the going was hard, both on the score sheet and psychologically.

The sad feature of these events is not so much the rights and wrongs of the case but that the disagreement between the West Indian Board of Control and her most famous son should have been allowed to occur. Not for the first time the Board were indecisive. They left their decision about who was to take over the captaincy very late. They could have told Gary publicly before the start of the Australian tour that they did not consider it fair to himself or the West Indies to subject him to the considerable physical strains of a five-day Test, after his long lay-off, unless he had taken part in a given number of first-class and club matches. This would have put the onus on Gary to prove his fitness and form in the middle. Looking at his record for West Indian cricket, one cannot help feeling he deserved such courtesy.

The Board tried to compromise and failed. Gary flew back to play for Notts before the Australians had even completed their Caribbean tour. With just a little early thought, it could all so easily have been avoided.

Anyone who doubts the difference Gary would have made to the West Indies' chances against the Australians a few months earlier, had their selectors been willing to accept his own assessment that he was fit, should read what the Editor of *Wisden* has to say on the series against England the same year:

There can be no two opinions that the presence of

Garfield Sobers was the main cause for the West Indies regaining their former glory. Before the party to tour England was considered, Sobers, because of a troublesome knee injury, from which he was recovering, following an operation, informed the selectors that he preferred to play the whole summer for Nottinghamshire, although he would be available for the three Tests if required.

The main reason why he did not wish to be considered for that tour was, of course, the treatment that had been meted out to him by the selectors in the West Indies.

Mishaps to two opening batsmen after the side reached England opened the way for Sobers's recall.

He was a great success in all three. In five innings he scored 10 and 51, 23 and 74, and 150. He also took three wickets in each of the first two Tests and at Lord's he equalled a Test record by holding six catches in the match. I have seen Sobers tear an attack apart in many wonderful batting displays, but for a well controlled and disciplined exhibition of brilliant strokes, coupled with sound defence, that 150 at Lord's portrayed the true master. And it must be remembered that his reliable slip fielding was another asset he brought to the side, for they had put down chances galore when facing Australia without him.

All in all, not a bad series for a man with a slight limp who was coming toward the end of his career. Yet if the West Indies had not suffered those two early injuries he might not have been invited for the Tests and would in all probability never have represented the West Indies again. Selectors have been known to err.

With Sobers around the new-look team slaughtered England. An important casualty in England's rout was their captain, Ray Illingworth. He was cast aside like a football manager whose club is unsuccessful.

Although Gary showed in England and in the ensuing series in the Caribbean against the same opponents that he was still a world-calibre cricketer – and backed up the claim with figures to match – he had lost a little of his edge and appetite, which serves as a reminder of just how good he was at his zenith.

That MCC drew the series in the West Indies came as a pleasant surprise after their poor showing in the series in England. It was, however, a false reflection on the merits of the two contestants. England were twice lucky to avoid defeat and in the final meeting levelled the series thanks almost entirely to the efforts of Boycott with the bat and Greig with the ball.

Gary played in the first three Tests, cried off the fourth because he felt tired, and the fifth was the end of the line for him. He took part in it, but then announced his retirement from first-class cricket.

Curiously, considering the perfection of the pitches in the series and the distinctly mundane English attack, Gary did not score as many runs as might have been expected. There was to be no final blaze of glory, because by the time he reached the crease the West Indies total was usually already so formidable that runs were not all that important, and Gary has always responded best to a real challenge. He liked providing runs when they were urgently required, not when they were there for the plucking. However, he put in some fine spells of bowling, which brought him 14 wickets in his four Tests, and his figures did not always do him justice.

In this, his last series, he was beginning to find cricket an effort, which is reflected in his withdrawal from the fourth Test in Guyana. To someone who had always enjoyed the sport, especially internationals, it was a clear indication that the time had come to quit the first-class scene. This was the right decision, although it would have been nice had he been able to play in the final of the Prudential World Cup of which the West Indies, to whom he gave so much, became the first winners at Lord's in 1975. He would still have been an automatic choice for them, but, alas, a minor injury, incurred while playing in his final full season of League cricket, caused him to withdraw just before the start of that unique knock-out tournament between eight countries.

16

Sobers on Cricket

Gary knows his cricket, which he has studied with care ever since he was at school. His views on the game are those of a man who, having spent over twenty years thinking about and playing cricket at the very highest level, has probably forgotten more than the majority will ever know. Unlike some outstanding cricketers he also possesses a keenly developed cricket brain. His opinions are consequently worth airing.

As a bowler he learned to pick out the weaknesses of opposing batsmen at a very early age – an essential tactical asset when he came to captain teams. It enabled him to make vital adjustments in the field immediately, like stationing mid-off a shade wider for the bottom-hand push-driver than he would be for a top-of-the-handle player with a full follow-through. He knew what type of bowling was most likely to unsettle a player, and acted accordingly. He read the game well, and though he preferred to be positive he was prepared to go on to the defensive when necessary.

As a batsman he acquired a defensive technique that was both correct and sound, while he quickly realised the importance of playing his attacking strokes off both front and back foot, along the ground, or deliberately lofted, with his bat kept perpendicular, and not swung across the line. He might angle the face of the bat to pierce the field, but he knew the value of keeping his downward swing and follow-through perfectly straight.

So which batsmen impressed Gary most? 'I like,' he says, 'a player who can destroy the bowling without looking as though he is going to get out.' In other words, players who are not only capable of making runs but also scoring them quickly and eloquently. He admires Ted Dexter, and thought Peter May a tremendous player. Although Colin Cowdrey had probably been as good and always appeared to have plenty of time to play his shots, Gary feels he has not dominated opposing attacks as often as his ability warranted. He has played against two other great English batsmen, Denis Compton and Sir Len Hutton, but it was too long ago for Gary to give a balanced judgment on them and it will be appreciated that he himself was an apprentice and a slow left-armer at that time. This meant that he was never able to see how they dealt with his seam and his wrist-spin.

Always a cricketing realist, Gary appreciates the advantages of having at least one accumulator in a batting line-up. Such a batsman will not destroy an attack, but he can be relied upon for runs. As a result he has a high regard for that arch-accumulator, Ken Barrington, but he feels that one of the weaknesses of English cricket is that it breeds too many 'grafters' and not enough stroke-makers.

This is borne out in the last two series against Ian Chappell's Australians, when only Tony Greig, who learned his cricket in South Africa, looked capable of dominating that formidable attack. It is also very noticeable that a high percentage of match-winning innings in both county championship and limited-over matches are made by overseas cricketers.

Gary blames the game's administrators and selectors at both county and national level for this marked shortage of stroke-makers. Coaches must also be prepared to accept some of the responsibility, with their attitude of 'You'd better cut that stroke out, it might cost you your wicket.' All too often selectors are inclined to choose dependable batsmen whose runs will take a long time coming rather than gamble on the uninhibited stroke-maker. Gary cites the case of Tom

Graveney, who was cast out of the national team into the wilderness for a considerable period while his place was filled by players who could never compare as stroke-makers. Similar stories can be told of numerous county sides, where the tendency is to include the batsman with runs in the book and the grafting technique, rather than taking a chance on an attacking prospect.

The young batsman soon realises this fact of cricketing life and, although he possesses the equipment to develop into an exciting stroke-maker, he may well decide to reduce his repertoire of strokes, eliminate as much risk as possible and graft for his runs, because these methods may well pay off, especially in the early stages when he is trying to establish himself in the team. This is what happened to Ken Barrington. Originally he was an attractive, free-scoring player with Surrey who was thrust into international cricket and then forgotten. Later he was recalled as a solid, ever-reliable run-accumulator with a rock-like defence – something he had forced himself to acquire. It would never have happened to an Australian or a West Indian.

At the end of the season when county committees decide on their retained list too much importance is placed on batting averages and not nearly enough emphasis on where and how the runs were made. The outcome is that the counties now have too many reliable, English-born batsmen who are dependable performers but whom nobody really wants to see bat, except when the demands of limited-over cricket or a particular situation have forced them to adopt a more aggressive approach.

Australian batsmen, though there have been many exceptions, like the legendary 'Slasher' Mackay, are generally more aggressive and score faster than their English counterparts. It therefore follows that, though Gary has seen less of their outstanding players than he has of the English, he admires them more. The powerful Peter Burge is a great favourite of Gary's, as is Doug Walters – except in England, where he has done himself less than justice. Gary rates both the Chappell brothers very highly; Greg, of course, is the master craftsman, but Gary feels that Ian is a more talented performer than is sometimes appreciated. The cutting and hooking of Keith Stackpole has left a lasting impression, while another formidable stroke-maker for whom Gary has a high regard is Norman O'Neill.

It is difficult to think of any outstanding West Indian batsman who at his best was ever less than entertaining. This does not mean they were incapable of producing a defensive innings when required but by nature and inclination they were essentially stroke-makers. Because they possessed the ability to score off a good delivery without undue risk and with an orthodox stroke they could dominate an opposing attack.

Gary holds a considerable number of West Indian batsmen in high esteem. Of the three W's he puts Everton Weekes first, perhaps because he was also his childhood idol. The dynamic Clive Lloyd at his best is very like Gary: certainly it would be difficult to decide who hit the ball harder. In the same way Alvin Kallicharran is a left-handed reproduction of the immensely graceful and talented Rohan Kanhai, two batsmen for whom Gary has nothing but praise. To those should be added Seymour Nurse, Basil Butcher, Conrad Hunte and Lawrence Rowe.

The West Indies have the knack of finding batsmen who are both effective – in that they make runs – and exciting – in that they are also entertainers. It is interesting, however, to note that West Indians have often been seriously troubled by a top-class leg-spinner, and Gary himself was no exception. Benaud, Tribe, Gupte and Gleason have all from time to time set him problems, while Bob Barber, not the most enthusiastic of bowlers, was keen to have a go at him at the start of his innings. This being the case, I asked Gary why the West Indies have produced so few leg-break and googly bowlers since the war, especially when it is remembered that the Caribbean pitches provide them with more bounce than in England. He thinks the main reason is that it takes a considerable time to become even an adequate wrist-spinner, and in the early stages such a bowler is probably inaccurate. This means that he is liable to be heavily punished by batsmen who have always dealt harshly with anything loose. In addition, county grounds often have small boundaries, which does not help. As a result many such bowlers have turned to other forms of bowling easier to control before attaining senior club cricket status.

As one would expect from someone who was granted the opportunity of playing first-class cricket at an early age, Gary believes in giving young players a chance. He feels that West Indian selectors are inclined to wait too long. As he puts it, 'It is all very well for them to say that so-and-so needs more experience, but the best place for him to gain this is out in the middle with the Island eleven.' This reluctance to gamble on the young is even more noticeable in England, where people are selected so late that anyone under twenty-five tends to be regarded as a youngster!

Although Gary is a great advocate of pushing teenagers on the basis that if they are good enough they are old enough – and one will never find out their worth until they are given the opportunity to show it at top level – he does not think the young are as keen as when he was a boy. When he found something was not going as it should he worked at it until it did. This dedicated approach appears to be on the decline.

Gary knows from personal experience that there is no automatic way to succeed at cricket. It has to be the result of hard, continual practice. Although his own basic batting technique is very straight and correct, Gary was never coached. He learned by watching others and then trying out what he had seen. As a result he is sceptical about some forms of coaching, especially coaching done *en masse*. On the other hand, he places considerable value on nets. This may seem strange, coming from someone who was not a great net enthusiast himself. 'For the first ten years of one's career net practice is very good,' he explained, 'but after that it is better to save one's energy and concentration for the middle.' In the latter part of his career he would just have the very occasional net, which is a very different approach, say, to that of Geoff Boycott who can never have enough of them.

To say that Gary considers all bowlers as potential cannon-fodder might suggest arrogance, which is not the case. Nevertheless, this is exactly what they were to him once he was set on a true pitch. There is a delightful example of this, which took place during a Warwickshire versus Notts match. Gary had just come to the crease and was having a look at the bowling. Lance Gibbs was in the middle of an over, and Rohan was providing him with some advice. 'Push two through flat and then throw one up, Gary won't be able to resist the challenge.' Lance, however, was slightly worried exactly what might happen to the one he tossed up, but eventually decided to follow Rohan's suggestion and bait the trap. Rohan was right in his prediction, but not in the way he intended. The two flat deliveries were met by a forward defensive, and then Gary went down the pitch to the flighted one. The ball was driven out of the ground. Lance sighed and Rohan departed quietly to the deep.

If bowlers have not impressed Gary over-much, one exception is Alan Davidson, who in the 1965 tour of the West Indies bowled beautifully, until he twisted his ankle. Gary also developed a healthy respect for Fred Trueman, who, although not as accurate as Brian Statham, gave him more trouble over the years. Another outstanding pair of fast bowlers in Gary's opinion – and in many others' – are Wes Hall and Charlie Griffith, for whom he took so many catches in the slips. However, he can never fully understand why so few English batsmen attempted to counterattack with the hook. He has a high regard for Tony Lock, who was never simply content to try to close up the game, as so many English spinners attempt to do on an easy wicket, but was always trying to pose problems. He is, of course, thinking here of Tony Lock in his third phase, after he had abandoned that dubious action which had enabled him to bowl spinners at a pace close to medium, and included a faster ball which was genuinely quick. Of the wrist-spinners he encountered he thought Subhash Gupte to be the best, but had a high regard for Richie Benaud, George Tribe and Jackie Gleason.

The five skippers whom Gary picked out for their ability make an interesting comparison because they were all different in their approach. The quintet consisted of Frank Worrell, two Australians and – in some respects surprisingly – two Yorkshiremen. The Australian pair were the intelligent, highly articulate and diplomatic Richie Benaud, who was very tough underneath the charm, and the more abrasive and frequently undiplomatic Ian Chappell. The two Yorkshiremen were Brian Close and Ray Illingworth, who with their common background took their cricket seriously and gave nothing away. However, it is not always appreciated that beneath the strokes and the laughter these same two qualities are very much in evidence in West Indian cricket, and never more so than in Barbados. That is why Gary holds these two Yorkshiremen in such esteem. He thought Brian an especially able attacking captain with a happy knack of doing the unexpected and seeing it come off, while it was Ray's clever and calculated tactical employment of those under him which appealed.

The first of the jet-set cricketers, Gary has taken part in top-class cricket in more parts of the world than anybody, and he has experienced a wide range of umpires. Like everybody who has played international cricket over a considerable period, he appreciates how important and how difficult their job is.

His view is that the over-all standard of umpiring is higher in England than anywhere else, which does not mean that there are not some outstanding umpires in other parts of the world, or that there are not some poor ones in England, but the English umpires have one enormous advantage over all the others. They are professionals. They have to stand every day, and many of them have also gained from the experience of having previously spent years in the game as players. They might not gain full marks in written examinations on the subject, but when it comes to deciding whether a lifting ball has flicked the shirt or the glove they are able to rely on instinct as well as eyesight.

Gary confirms what I have suspected during my recent visits to the Caribbean, that the standard of umpiring has improved enormously in the last five years. We would both rate D. Sang Hue and A. D. Jordan fit to stand in any company.

I asked Gary to name some changes he would like to see made to the present way cricket is played. He said:

'There are two rules that should be scrapped. First, the artificial limitation of the first innings of a county match to a hundred overs. This is intended to increase the tempo, but what happens on all too many occasions is that bowlers, knowing that they cannot be kept in the field for more than the time it takes to send down a hundred overs, will often, on good pitches, stop trying to get the batsmen out and simply try to stop him scoring, which is bad for cricket and for the spectator. This approach also often leads to youngsters being forced to slog in an effort to pick up bonus points, instead of settling down to building up an innings.

'Second, I do not agree with the limitation of only two men behind the bat on the leg side, because this unfairly penalises the good inswing bowler and also, on occasion, the off-spinner. The inswinger with a new ball needs at least two leg slips, plus a deep fine leg to cover the snick and also to guard against those batsmen who automatically use the "pick up" off the legs if there are only two close fieldsmen behind the bat. On a turning wicket the off-spinner usually requires two backward short legs and another man back to counter the sweep.

'I found with Notts that we played too much cricket and even I became slightly bored on occasion. When you don't really want to play, and are not looking forward to the game, it takes extra effort and this is likely to be shown in the cricket played.

'What I think would be good for the players, the spectators and English cricket is for a county to play one four-day match per week and the required number of one-day games. In a three-day match on a good wicket there are too many declarations, which has in turn led to limited overs in order to get results. These are necessary in one-day matches, but are bad for first-class cricket. In a four-day game there is a good chance, especially in England, of obtaining a positive result without declarations. It would also help bring more spinners back, which I think is very necessary. At the moment we are seeing far too much seam bowling in all types of cricket.

'I would also like to see fast and fast medium bowlers using shorter run-ups. Something is wrong when there are bowlers who are considerably slower than I was in the early Sixties, running more than three times as far as I did. It is absurd and time-consuming.'

Although Gary enjoyed and was ideally suited to one-day limited-over cricket, he is also aware of its disadvantages. I asked him for his thoughts on the World Cup and its future. Gary said, 'I think it makes a pleasant change and it gives spectators a chance of having a look at a large number of

This is Your Life

39 (*above*) Mrs Thelma Sobers during the programme on Gary in 1975. **40** Gary with one of his chief mentors, Garnett Ashby. **41** (*below*) . . . and with two of his brothers, George and Gerry.

42 Gary's slowest 76 ever : with a handicap c 5 he takes 3½ hours to go round the Victoria golf course in Australia.

43 Her Majesty the Queen confers a knighthood on Gary Sobers in 1975. The Duke of Edinburgh looks on.

very good players in a short period. If it is run as well as the first one in England in 1975, it should also continue to be a financial success, at least for as long as the sponsor, the Prudential Insurance Company, consider their expenditure justified.

'But although the money raised in this manner is welcome and wanted by cricket, I do not think that the one-day limited-over game is in the long run good for the game. It is clearly a fine spectator sport, but there should not be too much of it.

'I much prefer playing cricket where the prime objective of the bowler is to get the batsman out, as distinct from keeping him quiet, and in consequence often achieving the same objective. Limited-over cricket has done nothing to improve Test match cricket, except possibly the running between the wickets. I want to see batsmen able to make hundreds and two hundreds – and think this is what crowds also like to watch, providing such batting is the outcome of positive cricket.

'Although there is a need and a demand for one-day matches, cricket itself will be the loser if it is ever allowed to take the place of the highest form of the game – the Tests.'

17

Sir Gary – and the Future

Before the 1975 World Cup, Gary was to receive the supreme
accolade which can be awarded to any British sportsman. In
February of that year he was knighted by Her Majesty the
Queen. To make the event even more special, the ceremony
took place in Barbados, only a few miles from the house
where Gary was born. He thus joined two other great
cricketing knights, Sir Donald Bradman and Sir Len Hutton,
and two former West Indian cricketers, the late Sir Frank
Worrell and the late Sir Learie Constantine.

The names of some sportsmen who have been included in
the Honours List have been at times bizarre, and one
wonders how they qualified. There have also been some
glaring omissions – did not Peter May captain England
rather well for a long time, score a few runs not unattrac-
tively, and, in the West Indies, once continued playing with a
wound that needed hospitalisation? Yet no cricketer who
has had the privilege of playing with Gary would begrudge
him his knighthood. Unsurpassed as an all-rounder, he has
always played cricket the way the gods intended – absolutely
straight, absolutely hard, but never with malice.

Retirement often poses difficult problems for professional
cricketers. Their playing lives frequently stretch into their
late thirties or early forties, which is late to be starting a new
career. Also cricket, when compared with tennis, golf and
soccer and the rewards they can offer their star performers,
is badly paid. It provides a pleasing life-style, especially for
the unmarried man; but it provides little in the way of cash
returns (although tax-free Benefits can help considerably).

Finally, a high percentage of cricketers have few or no qualifications outside the game – which is hardly surprising, as many turn professional immediately on leaving school.

All these factors applied to Gary, only more so. Although, as a cricketing mercenary, he earned higher wages than the average English county professional, he was also forced to lead a far more nomadic existence. Many county players use the winter months when they are not on tour not only to earn extra money but to take up positions that could prove of use in the future. In Gary's case he was virtually on the move for twenty years without ever having a settled home. In addition to the West Indian tours and home series – which in his case entailed additional travelling – he took part in numerous unofficial tours, to nearly every country in the world where the game of cricket is played. He also engaged in State, County, Inter-Island and League cricket.

Thus, from the moment that Gary left school, cricket has been his main love and also virtually his sole source of income – although naturally there have been spin-offs, such as autographed bats. There are no regrets on that score: cricket has given Gary success, fame, and, if not a fortune, a very good standard of living. It has also enabled him to see the world, meet people and broaden his outlook.

Nonetheless, Gary's constant movement and activity has meant that he has had neither the time nor really the inclination to think overmuch about his future. Yet in one respect, for a West Indian cricketer, he has been very fortunate. The Barbados Cricket Association recognised his services and granted him a Benefit in 1973; this included a highly successful Knock-Out Tournament. An eleven-strong organising committee was formed, and they never missed a trick of any kind. Eric Innis, Ian Clarke, Peter Short, Ben Hoyos, Keith Walcott, Wes Hall, Rawle Brancker, John Dibbs, John Oxley, Les deBeger and Arthur Bethell make a powerful team, and they did an outstanding job. Barbados is not a large island and is very far from being a wealthy one, yet the Benefit raised the enormous sum of £17,000, easily a record for a West Indian cricketer.

I asked Ian Clarke, one of the organising committee, and a busy man who has an important post with Banks Breweries, why he had gone to so much trouble. 'I like Gary,' he said simply. He also recalled that in the early days when Banks Breweries were establishing themselves they had used Gary to publicise their beer. It was on a commercial basis, but when they ran into some financial problems Gary immediately waived his payment.

The West Indian player residing in the Caribbean will receive payment for both Island and Test matches, but there is no professional cricket as we understand it in England – which is, of course, why so many West Indian players are anxious to play in English League cricket. If they are good enough they can live on their income as a professional, and living in England normally also improves their standard of living. If they are international cricketers then the West Indian Board of Control will pay them their passage back home and provide them with wages during a Test series. It therefore follows that the West Indian cricketers who make the most money out of the game are the current Test and English county players. However, none so far has ever had a Benefit of anything approaching Gary's.

What of the future? There is no immediate problem. Gary has joined the Barbadian branch of a large Jamaican firm, The National Continental Corporation. He is also to take up an appointment with Slazengers, the British sports firm, who already have his autograph on many of their bats. The Slazengers connection was originally made in 1957, when I was working for them, and was asked to recommend some West Indian cricketers that might be taken on. The three W's were not available, so I suggested Gary, Collie Smith and Rohan Kanhai, who were then up-and-coming; all three duly joined the Slazenger team.

Apart from these business interests and Gary's realisation that he must master marketing and sales techniques, he wants to make some practical contribution to the game itself. He has no desire to become a coach, but his vast knowledge of cricket would make him an ideal selector. He would probably be most effective if given complete control and responsibility, as Don Revie has with the England football team. Being a member of a selection committee without having the final say might be restrictive and frustrating for him. All too often cricket selection committees – like all committees – depend too much on compromise. Although not arrogant in the normal sense of the word, Gary has very decided views on the game, which he is convinced are absolutely right. He is also too honest to agree to the inclusion of somebody who in his opinion was not the best person for the job and was nominated merely as a matter of diplomatic expediency.

The West Indian Selection Committee has always been handicapped by the rivalries between the islands, and these still exist. As a result, from time to time a player is included more because of where he comes from than because of his ability. Although an individual selector may be willing to see a touring party chosen without any player from his own island, he knows only too well the outcry it will cause at home. It would be like picking a football eleven for the whole of Great Britain and not including a Scotsman – only worse, because it is a racing certainty that in the West Indies a politician would seize the chance to add his voice to the general clamour.

If not cricket, Gary could always develop his golfing talents. He was good enough an all-round player to be picked for Barbados, and one of his colleagues in the golf team believes that he might have been even better had he been forced to work harder at the fundamentals. But it is difficult to suggest to somebody who is regularly belting the ball some 300 yards straight down the middle that his swing is not sufficiently grooved and disciplined!

Gary started to play golf in Australia in 1961 and found, like every game he took up, that it came easily and naturally to him. In a very short time he was able to hold his own with the many good golfing cricketers – as distinct from the numerous cricketing bandits who, with a high handicap yet with considerable natural ability, are to be found prowling the golf courses of the world.

In Australia Gary found the time and the opportunity for plenty of golf, but in England there was less of both available, and he was also having to play more cricket, so that in 1965 he gave up the sport. However, in 1968 when he found himself permanently based for long periods he took it up again and he is now a dedicated enthusiast with a low single-figure handicap – and a doughty competitor.

There have been those who have maintained that golf and cricket do not mix and that it harms batting, while most bowlers are more inclined to put their feet up on a rest day rather than trudge round a golf course. Gary, Hutton, Dexter, Cowdrey and Compton are just some of the many cricketers who have found that golf has not harmed their batting. Len Hutton, indeed, was convinced that far from harming a batsman it was a positive benefit. He suggested that I should take golf up seriously, because he felt it would improve my driving, but he had never seen me on a golf course. Which was just as well.

Who are the outstanding cricketer-golfers? One's mind instinctively goes to Leonard Crawley, a brilliant amateur golfer who became both an outstanding writer and critic on the game, but before the war was also a very dashing batsman for Essex, who many believe could have developed into an international player, had he not concentrated on the small ball game.

Of the post-war group of international cricketers who were also fine golfers Ted Dexter, who gained a Cambridge Blue at it, is generally considered the best. If he had concentrated on the little white ball game he must surely at the very least have become a Walker-Cup regular.

For sheer elegance of style Tom Graveney, whom I once saw go round the Royal Melbourne Club in one over par, probably leads the field, and he is another who could well have gone far in the world of golf. Ken Barrington, who has applied himself to his new love with the same dedication that he did to his batting, is a much-respected performer because of his reliability.

Colin Cowdrey is another low-handicap golfer, and nobody would beat Brian Close if the strokes had to be taken alternatively left- and right-handed. However, now that Gary has retired from cricket and providing time allows, he may well eclipse them all.

It may seem out of place to be talking about golf at the end of a book about the most complete cricketer of all time. But Gary's potential and natural aptitude are so high in this new sphere that he might even be capable of making a real impact on the golf course.

Although Gary is keenly interested in West Indian politics, at the moment he has no leanings toward being a politician. Nonetheless, it will come as no surprise if one day he were persuaded to change his mind. His escutcheon is unblemished, and his personal standing throughout the Caribbean and in Barbados in particular is exceptionally high. Gary is still only forty, and has almost another lifetime to conquer fresh fields. With his easy charm, he might develop into a fine ambassador. His honesty might cause problems; but that in itself would make a pleasant change.

Chronology

best-ever all-round series, scoring 722 runs for an average of 103 and capturing 20 wickets.

1966–67   Tours India and wins series.

1968   England tour West Indies, and Gary scores magnificent century at Sabina Park on a bad pitch when West Indies close to defeat.

Signs on to play for Nottinghamshire.

1968–69   Tours Australia and New Zealand. Engaged to Pru Kirby.

1969   Captains short tour of England.

11 Sept.   Marries Pru.

1970   Captains Rest of the World against England in England.

Visits Rhodesia and returns home to controversy.

1971   Captains West Indies against India in the West Indies.
Birth of Matthew.

1971–72   Captains Rest of the World against Australia in Australia.

Captains West Indies against New Zealand in the West Indies.

Knee operation.

1973   Misses first Test Match for West Indies since début in 1954. West Indies lose series to Australia 3–0.

Returns to England to play for Notts. Is chosen to play in all three Tests against England under Rohan Kanhai.

1974   Plays in four Tests against England in the West Indies. His last Test in Trinidad. Announces his retirement from international cricket.

Birth of Daniel.

1975
February   Knighted in Barbados.

Plays League cricket for Littleborough, but injury prevents him taking part in the World Cup.

Career Statistics

CENTURIES (26)

v. Australia (4)
132 at Brisbane, 1960–61
168 at Sydney, 1960–61
110 at Adelaide, 1968–69
113 at Sydney, 1968–69

v. England (10)
226 at Bridgetown, 1959–60
147 at Kingston, 1959–60
145 at Georgetown, 1959–60
102 at Headingley, 1963
161 at Old Trafford, 1966
163* at Lord's, 1966
174 at Headingley, 1966
113* at Kingstown, 1967–68
152 at Georgetown, 1967–68
150* at Lord's, 1973

v. New Zealand (1)
142 at Bridgetown, 1971–72

v. Pakistan (3)
365* at Kingston, 1957–58
125 at Georgetown, 1957–58
(1st Innings)
109* at Georgetown, 1957–58
(2nd Innings)

v. India (8)
142* at Bombay, 1958–59
198 at Kanpur, 1958–59
106* at Calcutta, 1958–59
153 at Kingston, 1962
104 at Kingston, 1962
108* at Georgetown, 1971
178* at Bridgetown, 1971
132 at Port of Spain, 1971

* Indicates not out.

MAIN WICKET PARTNERSHIPS

179 for 4th wicket with C. L. Walcott v. Australia at Kingston, 1955
100 for 5th wicket with E. D. Weekes v. England at Lord's, 1957
446 for 2nd wicket with C. C. Hunte v. Pakistan at Kingston, 1957–58
269 for 2nd wicket with C. L. Walcott v. Pakistan at Georgetown, 1957–58
188* for 4th wicket with C. L. Walcott v. Pakistan at Kingston, 1957–58
135 for 2nd wicket with C. C. Hunte v. Pakistan at Georgetown, 1957–58
101 for 5th wicket with O. G. Smith v. Pakistan at Port of Spain, 1957–58

119 for 4th wicket with O. G. Smith v. India at Bombay, 1958–59
134* for 5th wicket with B. F. Butcher v. India at Bombay, 1958–59
114 for 5th wicket with B. F. Butcher v. India at Kanpur, 1958–59
163 for 6th wicket with J. Solomon v. India at Kanpur, 1958–59
160* for 6th wicket with J. Solomon v. India at Calcutta, 1958–59
162 for 3rd wicket with R. B. Kanhai v. Pakistan at Lahore, 1958–59
399 for 4th wicket with F. M. Worrell v. England at Bridgetown, 1959–60
115 for 3rd wicket with R. B. Kanhai v. England at Georgetown, 1959–60
121 for 5th wicket with F. M. Worrell v. England at Georgetown, 1959–60
133 for 3rd wicket with E. McMorris v. England at Kingston, 1959–60 (McMorris retired hurt and the stand continued with S. M. Nurse for 110 more runs)
174 for 4th wicket with F. M. Worrell v. Australia at Brisbane, 1960–61
128 for 5th wicket with S. M. Nurse v. Australia at Sydney, 1960–61
110 for 6th wicket with F. M. Worrell v. India at Kingston, 1962
127 for 7th wicket with I. Mendonca v. India at Kingston, 1962
120 for 4th wicket with C. C. Hunte v. England at Old Trafford, 1963
143 for 4th wicket with R. B. Kanhai v. England at Headingley, 1963
160 for 4th wicket with B. F. Butcher v. Australia at Port of Spain, 1965
127 for 6th wicket with D. A. J. Holford v. England at Old Trafford, 1966
274* for 6th wicket with D. A. J. Holford v. England at Lord's, 1966
173 for 5th wicket with B. F. Butcher v. England at Trent Bridge, 1966
265 for 5th wicket with S. M. Nurse v. England at Headingley, 1966
122 for 5th wicket with R. B. Kanhai v. England at The Oval, 1966
102* for 5th wicket with C. H. Lloyd v. India at Bombay, 1966–67
110 for 6th wicket with D. A. J. Holford v. England at Kingston, 1967–68
63* for 9th wicket with W. W. Hall v. England at Port of Spain, 1967–68
250 for 4th wicket with R. B. Kanhai v. England at Georgetown, 1967–68
134 for 5th wicket with S. M. Nurse v. Australia at Melbourne, 1968–69
118 for 6th wicket with S. M. Nurse v. Australia at Sydney, 1968–69
173 for 4th wicket with R. B. Kanhai v. India at Kingston, 1971
170* for 4th wicket with C. A. Davis v. India at Georgetown, 1971
167 for 4th wicket with C. A. Davis v. India at Bridgetown, 1971
107* for 6th wicket with J. N. Shepherd v. India at Bridgetown, 1971
177 for 5th wicket with C. A. Davis v. India at Port of Spain, 1971
254 for 6th wicket with C. A. Davis v. New Zealand at Bridgetown, 1971–72

155* for 7th wicket with B. D. Julien v. England at Lord's, 1973
(Sobers retired with a stomach upset and the stand continued
with K. D. Boyce for 76 more runs; Sobers returned to make
150)

112 for 6th wicket with B. D. Julien v. England at Kingston, 1974

* stand unfinished.

BEST BOWLING

5 for 120 runs v. Australia at Melbourne, 1960–61
5 for 63 runs v. India at Kingston, 1962
5 for 60 runs v. England at Edgbaston, 1963
5 for 41 runs v. England at Headingley, 1966
6 for 73 runs v. Australia at Brisbane, 1968–69
5 for 42 runs v. England at Headingley, 1969.

FOR THE REST OF THE WORLD
v. ENGLAND, 1970

BATTING

Matches	Inns.	Not Outs	Runs	Highest Inns.	100's	50's	Average	Catches
5	9	1	588	183	2	3	73.50	7

BOWLING

Matches	Balls	Maidens	Runs	Wickets	5 wkts. in Innings	Average
5	1636	106	452	21	1	21.52

CENTURIES (2)	BEST PARTNERSHIPS	BEST BOWLING
183 at Lord's	198 for 7th wicket	6 for 21 runs at
114 at Headingley	with Intikhab Alam at Lord's	Lord's
	155 for 5th wicket	
	with C. H. Lloyd at Edgbaston	
	165 for 5th wicket	
	with R. G. Pollock at The Oval	

FOR THE REST OF THE WORLD
v. AUSTRALIA, 1971–72

BATTING

Matches	Inns.	Not Outs	Runs	Highest Inns.	100's	50's	Average	Catches
5	9	2	341	254	1	0	48·71	2

BOWLING

Matches	Balls	Maidens	Runs	Wickets	5 wkts. in Innings	Average
5	822	7	485	9	0	48·38

CENTURIES   BEST PARTNERSHIPS   BEST BOWLING
254 at Melbourne   ——   ——

G. S. SOBERS IN TEST CRICKET FOR WEST INDIES

Season	Against	Matches	Inns.	Not Outs	Runs	Highest Inns.	100's	50's	Average	Catches
1953–54	England	1	2	1	40	26	0	0	40.00	0
1955	Australia	4	8	2	231	64	0	1	38.50	1
1956	New Zealand	4	5	0	81	27	0	0	16.20	5
1957	England	5	10	0	320	66	0	2	32.00	1
1957–58	Pakistan	5	8	2	824	365*	3	3	137.33	2
1958–59	India	5	8	2	557	198	3	0	92.83	5
1958–59	Pakistan	3	5	0	160	72	0	1	32.00	2
1959–60	England	5	8	1	709	226	3	1	101.28	7
1960–61	Australia	5	10	0	430	168	2	1	43.00	12
1962	India	5	7	1	424	153	2	1	70.66	11
1963	England	5	8	0	322	102	1	2	40.25	8
1965	Australia	5	10	1	352	69	0	2	39.11	8
1966	England	5	8	1	722	174	3	2	103.14	10
1966–67	India	3	5	2	342	95	0	5	114.00	7
1967–68	England	5	9	3	545	152	2	2	90.83	4
1968–69	Australia	5	10	0	497	113	2	2	49.70	6
1968–69	New Zealand	3	5	0	70	39	0	0	14.00	5
1969	England	3	6	1	150	50*	0	1	30.00	2
1971	India	5	10	2	597	178*	3	1	74.62	4
1971–72	New Zealand	5	8	1	253	142	1	0	36.14	2
1973	England	3	5	1	306	150*	1	2	76.50	7
1974	England	4	5	0	100	57	0	1	20.00	1
	Totals	93	160	21	8032	365*	26	30	57.78	110

Mode of Dismissal:—Bowled 34, caught 79, lbw 16, stumped 1, run out 9. Total 139.

* *Indicates not out.*

SOBERS'S FULL RECORD IN TEST CRICKET

(Including 'Tests' for Rest of the World XI)

BATTING

Matches	Inns.	Not Outs	Runs	Highest Inns.	100's	50's	Average	Catches
98	169	22	8620	365*	28	33	58.63	117

BOWLING

Matches	Balls	Maidens	Runs	Wickets	5 wkts. in Innings	Average
98	23235	1079	8451	256	7	33.01

BOWLING FOR WEST INDIES

Season	Against	Matches	Balls	Maidens	Runs	Wickets	5 wkts. in Innings	Average
1953–54	England	1	179	9	81	4	0	20.25
1955	Australia	4	563	36	213	6	0	35.50
1956	New Zealand	4	281	26	49	2	0	24.50
1957	England	5	804	24	355	5	0	71.00
1957–58	Pakistan	5	1029	53	377	4	0	94.25
1958–59	India	5	715	33	292	10	0	29.20
1958–59	Pakistan	3	396	36	77	0	0	—
1959–60	England	5	684	14	355	9	0	39.44
1960–61	Australia	5	1528	27	588	15	1	39.20

Year	Opponent				Runs	Wkts	Average	5w
1962	India	5	1341	61	473	23	20.56	1
1963	England	5	1386	50	571	20	28.55	1
1965	Australia	5	1155	53	490	12	40.83	0
1966	England	5	1618	78	545	20	27.25	1
1966–67	India	3	931	51	350	14	25.00	0
1967–68	England	5	1397	72	508	13	39.07	0
1968–69	Australia	5	1649	37	733	18	40.72	1
1968–69	New Zealand	3	840	23	301	7	43.00	0
1969	England	3	870	47	318	11	28.90	1
1971	India	5	1314	71	401	12	33.41	0
1971–72	New Zealand	5	1086	56	332	10	33.20	0
1973	England	3	493	24	169	6	28.16	0
1974	England	4	1340	92	421	14	30.07	0
Totals		93	21599	973	7999	235	34.03	6

How wickets were taken:—bowled 54, caught 137, LBW 38, stumped 6. Total 235.

BATTING FOR WEST INDIES

	Tests	Inns.	Not Outs	Runs	Highest Inns.	100's	50's	Average	Catches
v. England	36	61	8	3214	174	10	13	60.64	40
v. Australia	19	38	3	1510	168	4	6	43.14	27
v. New Zealand	12	18	1	404	142	1	0	23.76	12
v. India	18	30	7	1920	198	8	7	83.47	27
v. Pakistan	8	13	2	984	365*	3	4	89.45	4
Totals	93	160	21	8032	365*	26	30	57.78	110

* Indicates not out.

BOWLING FOR WEST INDIES

	Tests	Balls	Maidens	Runs	Wickets	5 Wkts. in Inns.	Average
v. England	36	8771	410	3323	102	3	32.57
v. Australia	19	4895	153	2024	51	2	39.68
v. New Zealand	12	2207	105	682	19	0	35.89
v. India	18	4301	216	1516	59	1	25.69
v. Pakistan	8	1425	89	454	4	0	113.50
Totals	93	21599	973	7999	235	6	34.03

BATTING FOR WEST INDIES

	Tests	Inns.	Not Outs	Runs	Highest Inns.	100's	50's	Average	Catches
In West Indies	44	75	14	4075	365*	14	12	66.80	40
In Australia	10	20	0	927	168	4	3	46.35	18
In England	21	37	3	1820	174	5	9	53.52	28
In India	8	13	4	899	198	3	5	99.88	12
In New Zealand	7	10	0	151	39	0	0	15.10	10
In Pakistan	3	5	0	160	72	0	1	32.00	2
Totals	93	160	21	8032	365*	26	30	57.78	110

BOWLING FOR WEST INDIES

	Tests	Balls	Maidens	Runs	Wickets	5 Wkts. in Inns.	Average
In West Indies	44	10088	517	3651	107	1	34.12
In Australia	10	3177	64	1321	33	2	40.03
In England	21	5171	223	1958	62	3	31.58
In India	8	1646	84	642	24	0	26.75
In New Zealand	7	1121	49	350	9	0	38.88
In Pakistan	3	396	36	77	0	0	—
Totals	93	21599	973	7999	235	6	34.03

BATTING ON WEST INDIAN GROUNDS

Ground	Tests	Inns.	Not Outs	Runs	Highest Inns.	100's	50's	Average	Catches
Bridgetown	9	14	2	914	226	3	3	76.16	9
Georgetown	7	12	3	853	145	5	1	94.77	5
Kingston	11	18	5	1354	365*	5	4	104.15	8
Port of Spain	17	31	4	954	132	1	4	35.33	18
Totals	44	75	14	4075	365*	14	12	66.80	40

BATTING ON AUSTRALIAN GROUNDS

Ground	Tests	Inns.	Not Outs	Runs	Highest Inns.	100's	50's	Average	Catches
Adelaide	2	4	0	183	110	1	1	45.75	4
Brisbane	2	4	0	184	132	1	0	46.00	4
Melbourne	3	6	0	180	67	0	2	30.00	6
Sydney	3	6	0	380	168	2	0	63.33	4
Totals	10	20	0	927	168	4	3	46.35	18

BATTING ON ENGLISH GROUNDS

Ground	Tests	Inns.	Not Outs	Runs	Highest Inns.	100's	50's	Average	Catches
Edgbaston	3	6	0	190	74	0	2	31.66	2
Headingley	4	7	0	374	174	2	1	53.42	2
Lord's	5	9	3	571	163*	2	2	95.16	8
Old Trafford	3	4	0	283	161	1	1	70.75	8
The Oval	4	7	0	249	81	0	2	35.57	3
Trent Bridge	2	4	0	153	94	0	1	38.25	5
Totals	21	37	3	1820	174	5	9	53.52	28

BATTING ON INDIAN GROUNDS

Ground	Tests	Inns.	Not Outs	Runs	Highest Inns.	100's	50's	Average	Catches
Bombay	2	4	2	270	142*	1	2	135.00	5
Calcutta	2	2	1	176	106*	1	1	176.00	2
Kanpur	1	2	0	202	198	1	0	101.00	0
Madras	2	4	1	207	95	0	2	69.00	5
New Delhi	1	1	0	44	44	0	0	44.00	0
Totals	8	13	4	899	198	3	5	99.88	12

BATTING ON NEW ZEALAND GROUNDS

Ground	Tests	Inns.	Not Outs	Runs	Highest Inns.	100's	50's	Average	Catches
Auckland	2	4	0	13	11	0	0	3.25	3
Christchurch	2	2	0	25	25	0	0	12.50	2
Dunedin	1	1	0	27	27	0	0	27.00	2
Wellington	2	3	0	86	39	0	0	28.66	3
Totals	7	10	0	151	39	0	0	15.10	10

BATTING ON PAKISTAN GROUNDS

Ground	Tests	Inns.	Not Outs	Runs	Highest Inns.	100's	50's	Average	Catches
Dacca	1	2	0	74	45	0	0	37.00	0
Karachi	1	2	0	14	14	0	0	7.00	0
Lahore	1	1	0	72	72	0	1	72.00	2
Totals	3	5	0	160	72	0	1	32.00	2

BOWLING ON WEST INDIAN GROUNDS

Ground	Tests	Balls	Maidens	Runs	Wickets	5 Wkts. in Inns.	Average
Bridgetown	9	2159	125	761	19	0	40.05
Georgetown	7	1680	94	577	20	0	28.85
Kingston	11	2390	116	879	27	1	32.55
Port of Spain	17	3859	182	1434	41	0	34.97
Totals	44	10088	517	3651	107	1	34.12

BOWLING ON AUSTRALIAN GROUNDS

Ground	Tests	Balls	Maidens	Runs	Wickets	5 Wkts. in Inns.	Average
Adelaide	2	904	19	364	7	0	52.00
Brisbane	2	702	17	248	9	1	27.55
Melbourne	3	859	14	337	10	1	33.70
Sydney	3	712	14	372	7	0	53.14
Totals	10	3177	64	1321	33	2	40.03

BOWLING ON ENGLISH GROUNDS

Ground	Tests	Balls	Maidens	Runs	Wickets	5 Wkts. in Inns.	Average
Edgbaston	3	750	25	300	10	1	30.00
Headingley	4	1024	42	374	19	2	19.68
Lord's	5	858	42	340	7	0	48.57
Old Trafford	3	822	35	338	8	0	42.25
The Oval	4	1111	55	385	12	0	32.08
Trent Bridge	2	606	24	221	6	0	36.83
Totals	21	5171	223	1958	62	3	31.58

BOWLING ON INDIAN GROUNDS

Ground	Tests	Balls	Maidens	Runs	Wickets	5 Wkts. in Inns.	Average
Bombay	2	348	15	152	5	0	30.40
Calcutta	2	341	18	141	9	0	15.66
Kanpur	1	270	14	91	2	0	45.50
Madras	2	543	34	192	8	0	24.00
New Delhi	1	144	3	66	0	0	—
Totals	8	1646	84	642	24	0	26.75

BOWLING ON NEW ZEALAND GROUNDS

Ground	Tests	Balls	Maidens	Runs	Wickets	5 Wkts. in Inns.	Average
Auckland	2	512	15	201	3	0	67.00
Christchurch	2	312	11	91	3	0	30.33
Dunedin	1	24	4	0	0	0	—
Wellington	2	273	19	58	3	0	19.33
Totals	7	1121	49	350	9	0	38.88

BOWLING ON PAKISTAN GROUNDS

Ground	Tests	Balls	Maidens	Runs	Wickets	5 Wkts. in Inns.	Average
Dacca	1	66	6	11	0	0	—
Karachi	1	294	29	57	0	0	—
Lahore	1	36	1	9	0	0	—
Totals	3	396	36	77	0	0	—

Index